NORMAN MAILER'S
THE DEER PARK

Books by Norman Mailer

The Naked and the Dead   *1948*

Barbary Shore   *1951*

The Deer Park (novel)   *1954*

The White Negro   *1957*

Advertisements For Myself   *1959*

Deaths For The Ladies (and other disasters)   *1962*

The Presidential Papers   *1963*

An American Dream   *1965*

Cannibals and Christians   *1966*

The Deer Park: A Play   *1967*

NORMAN MAILER'S THE DEER PARK

A PLAY

THE DIAL PRESS New York 1967

Library of Congress catalog card number: 67-16539
Printed in the United States of America
First printing, 1967
Design by Larry Kamp

ACKNOWLEDGMENTS:

Scenes 2, 3 and 4 originally appeared in *Advertisements
for Myself* by Norman Mailer; Copyright © 1959 by
Norman Mailer. Reprinted by
permission of G. P. Putnam's Sons.

Scenes 7 and 10 originally appeared in *Partisan Review*,
Fall 1959. Copyright 1959 by *Partisan Review*.
Reprinted by permission.

Part One of the Introduction originally appeared in
The New York Times. © 1967 by The New York Times
Company. Reprinted by permission.

To *Leo Garen* and *James E. Walsh*
Director and Producer
of

THE DEER PARK

and

To *Paul John Austin*—Stage Manager
and to the brave players in the first New York company
Rip Torn, Rosemary Tory and *Hugh Marlowe*
Will Lee, Beverly Bentley and *Mickey Knox*
Gene Lindsey and *Margaret Fairchild*
Mara Lynn and *Joe McWherter*
Marsha Mason and *Gary Campbell*
Bernard Farbar

and to the fine work of the technical crew
and the box office
and the standbys.

And to *Elizabeth Farley*
Richard Shepard
Dan Durning
and *Tom Baker*
for the first production of "The Deer Park"
at Act IV in Provincetown.

INTRODUCTION

I

NOT SO VERY LONG AGO the National Foundation on the Arts and Humanities had a symposium for an invited audience of newspaper critics. Conducted by Roger Stevens and Carolyn Kizer, the symposium was given the formal title of "What's Wrong with Criticism in the Performing Arts," and Session One took place in a conference room of the Whitney, with Arthur Schlesinger, Gerald Weales, Clive Barnes, William Phillips, Michael Smith of the *Village Voice,* and myself.

Now, it would be nice (and doubtless out of character) for me to describe which opinions were held by the others, and what shape was taken by colloquies between the speakers and the invited audience, but I cannot, for *The Deer Park* was already in rehearsal that day, and I rushed up to the Whitney for a half hour, said my piece somewhere toward the end of that three-hour conference, and was out again, on the way back to Christopher Street downtown in the Village and rehearsals at the De Lys. So I had only an inkling of what had gone before, but it was enough to improvise ten minutes of talk. Because what came through the echo of completed conversations was the old and essential antagonism of the artist in the theatre (the playwright, actor, director, yea, often the producer!) toward the cruel, rigorous, even unreasonable demand of the open-

7

ing night reviews, that cry of protest because all the years of writing, the months of preparation, and the repetitive soul-killing weeks of rehearsal must still come down to the electric hour when the drama reviewer sprints from the theatre, snatches his opening lead from the well-tuned bag of his wit, and is off to his desk, say, say, his guillotine. Three times out of four, nine times out of ten, the work is doomed. If it is an exciting, difficult play, imperfectly presented (as, for example, might be said of *Slow Dance on the Killing Ground*), then the odds are 19 out of 20 that the critic, the two or three or four good men inhabiting those nerve-festooned portals between the theatre and the public, will do the job in, and the play does not live.

We are all familiar with this profound plaint. But the correctives and/or the preventatives lack salt. Invariably they suggest that the critic see the play after it opens, that he take his time, that he brood upon the nature of what he has seen. All this, while sensible, is nonetheless depressing. That, in fact, is what I began to say at the symposium in the Whitney. For it seemed to me that the opening night review with all its inequities, yaws of judgment, its surrealistic surgeries upon esthetic value, is nonetheless indispensable to the theatre, and I would not enjoy writing a play and seeing it produced if I could not have an opening night before a full posse of critics. For that is also a part of the play. That is its dramatic edge, its confrontation with the history it will or not make. Those opening night reviews, written to the demand of fever speed, are a ritual at the heart of the drama. A professional theatre without the sense of crisis provided by opening night is like a marriage in city hall.

Yet what a huge price is paid for the excitement of the opening night review. The desire for success lucubrates secret prostitutions in the soul. Some are not so secret. A theatre whose economic foundations are built on the opinions of five or six men (now reduced to four men, or three men, or two, can it be even one man?) is a theatre whose esthetics must be built on the most anomalous mechanical principles—the intake pipe is on the outlet valve: the the-

8

atre becomes geared to the taste of the newspaper critic which is to say—not his taste, but his need. And his need —we can make no mistake here—is for simple plays.

A drama critic is a man of some integrity and discipline —he could not otherwise fulfill the professional rigors of his work. Like all men of integrity, he prefers to do a good job. A simple play offers just that opportunity. Its moral situations may be novel but they must be clearcut (go back to *The Moon Is Blue*), its characters are happiest when amusing or worthy of our compassion, but they cannot be too contradictory or complex. In a play with five characters, four preferably must be comfortable to the mind so that the play may concentrate on the fifth—perhaps I am thinking of *Come Back, Little Sheba*. It does not matter. Fifty plays a season, good, bad, magnificent, or atrocious, fulfill this formula. The simple play enables the reviewer to make his assessment on the evidence before him. He can mark the play precisely on the scale of his accumulated experience. The simple play—all else equal—inspires the critic therefore with a benevolent sensation; he can feel like a good man doing a good work of appraisal.

The only difficulty is that the simple play alienates the theatre from life, for in life, moral situations are rarely novel, but invariably overloaded with counterpoint, and the people who surround you are not always comfortable to the concepts of the mind; indeed, they often prove most depressing just at the moment when they are presumably most worthy of compassion. In contrast, the simple play provides a wish-fulfillment—it extracts a neat pattern from the flux of the unruly: it has, in consequence, as much to do with life, this simple play, as a hair-pin has to do with jewelry, but the hair-pin is what prospers, the hair-pin becomes nine-tenths of the stock in the jewelry store. The theatre roots itself in the simple. Actors learn to look for precise results, directors look for moments—call them tricks—since a simple play depends for its success on offering, let us say, one hundred moments of pleasure rather than 50, and playwrights develop an eye for linear mechanisms of plot which will lift them from the moral bogs of their theme.

9

It comes down to one thundering, if matter-of-fact difficulty: You cannot predict success for a play once it is sufficiently complex to need a night's sleep for comprehending it. Any dramatic theme which requires an audience to return to their unconscious later that night, in order to evaluate the depth of what is being said in the theater, is carrying a most ambitious monkey on its back, for the drama reviewer does not have the time to put the play together in his sleep and write about it in the morning. He must take it as it is, all confusion to the fore, deal with it in the same partial terms of comprehension that we feel when we meet a gallery of dazzlers, freaks, heroes, and creeps at a party and can't begin to divine what is going on until the morning after, not until our sleep has done the work of assembling a little more of what we have seen into some conjunction with the stiff-necked patterns of our mind.

These were my remarks at the symposium—these, more or less. I ended with some vague notions paraded forward about the possibility of existential criticism—a hint that the drama reviewer recognize the impossibility of reviewing difficult plays immediately, that he write for the morning daily, "No review today—it's too early to tell. I'll write about it in a week, and maybe I'll even go to see it again. Maybe I won't. Let us see. In the meantime, I suggest this play might just possibly be worth keeping alive."

We are asking for miracles, yes? We request the authority to relinquish his infallibility. A faint dream. The moment is not near. No, I was obviously making my plea with a particular play in mind—no accident that beneath the hat of the symposiast was the steel helmet of the playwright. I was thinking of *The Deer Park,* and its particular strengths and weaknesses, delights and *longueurs,* after ten stunning maniacally depressive days of rehearsal, and I was thinking as well of the monumental impossibility that any drama reviewer born could review this play to his own satisfaction (or mine!) an hour after he had seen it, when I had lived with the events, crises, and themes before me for near to 18 years, had worked on the play for ten, had rewritten it four times. It was by now perhaps the dearest work of all my work. There were times when I thought I even cared more for it than the novel from which it was delivered; it was certainly different from the novel, narrower, more harrowing, funnier I hoped, sadder, certainly more tragic. It was also more multi-layered. If I was a novelist trying to write plays, I was also trying to put more into this play than I had into the novel. If the compass was obligatorily more narrow, the well was being dug to a deeper water—I realized at one point that I had a work with 13 characters, and not one of these characters was unworthy of a play for himself. Indeed, it sometimes seemed to me that I had compressed ten plays into three hours.

There was an idiom in the theatre I could not bear. It was the one which brought all arms and aid to the lowest common denominator of the audience. I was tired of seeing plays which went along carefully, thoughtfully, and decently for two hours in order to arrive at a small but perfect dramatic explosion. Any audience which did not know all the steps from opening curtain to explosion was an audience not worth writing for, since the American public was by now finally saturated in plot, in genre, in situation, and the 20 stratagems of denouement. So why not write a play which went from explosion to explosion, or—since this is not the Fourth of July—from one moment of intensity or reality (which is to say a moment which feels more real than other moments) to the next—a play which went at full throttle all the way. Which is precisely what was done this summer when *The Deer Park,* a four-hour play, its third draft five years old, had an hour or more taken out of it, a transition which cut away all dramatic scaffolding, connective tissue, road signs, guides, and left the play stripped to its essential connections, the movement ideally from one real scene to the next, with the audience left to fill the spaces between, like the eye of the beholder face to face with a painting by Larry Rivers.

I had my play then with 13 wide open characters and a set of one hundred blackouts or quick scenes I called changes, quick as the cuts in a movie, for it seemed right to capture the dislocation of life in Hollywood by a play which played like a movie—although not quite! Wait until you see! And I was pleased. For the play occupied a space which had been left uninhabited too long, that area between the explorations of the realistic play and that electric sense of transition which lives in the interruptions and symbols of the Theatre of the Absurd. *The Deer Park* was conceived to live in the land between. It was—could you term it so?—an existential play. A surrealistic comedy about the nature of tragedy I called it once in a fatuous moment. For I was trying to tell in this play something of what I knew about sex and love, and no theme—here comes our paradox—is more difficult to present in the theater. None more difficult, because—dear reader—there is a no man's land between sex and love, and it alters in the night.

We go to sleep convinced we are in one state, we awaken in the other, and murderous emotions patrol the ever-changing line of no man's land. You do not write a play about sex and love which is a simple play, a situation comedy, a switcheroo of slamming doors and lovers under beds, no, rather you try to induce an existence which is like an animal or a beast or a beautiful woman, a being which breathes and is mysterious and not altogether accessible and changes all the time. Ideally, it stays fascinating, then haunting, it is a play to which you go back, a play with which you fall in love, a bitch, tears of blood in her heart, the perfume of the Indies in her flanks.

We are at the core of the comic, are we not? A playwright in love with his play. It calls for Voltaire, Shaw, or our own Albee to delineate it. Stick in the needles. Bring forth the pots. Lay on the acid. This playwright is ready to burn for the love of his own dramàtic work. There were too many years when he dreamed of *The Deer Park* on Broadway and the greatest first night of the decade, too many hours of rage when he declaimed to himself that his play was as good as *Death of a Salesman,* or even, and here he gulped hard, *A Streetcar Named Desire.* Yes, his play was there, so he felt. Then years went by, and experi-

12

ence was gained in the theatre and knowledge that a play like *Streetcar* was a miracle, and angels without dollars must also have helped it on its way. Finally the playwright learned that if he would see his play at all, and see it right, he would see it in that land below Broadway, in the terrain of a true turf, the Village, at a jewel-box in red velvet (red velvet at least was there) called the Theatre De Lys, the theatre of the lily, yes, and there Off-Broadway it would have a chance to live, perhaps there it could survive those opening night reviews the playwright was certain could not be steeped in joy, and he studied the play in rehearsal and hoped *The Deer Park* was really as good as he believed, for then he could read any review, that would not be hard, for when you know the work is good there is a particular sweetness to the sad taste with which you imbibe negative opinions of yourself. But, dear readers, I let you in on a secret—there have also been moments in rehearsal when I have said to myself, "Dear Messieurs Chapman, Kerr, Nadel and Watts—if you do not like my play, what horror if I am obliged to agree with you."

On the other hand, there have been moments of magic when the dialogue and the action and the set—but we have bragged enough about this theatrical baby. Here is a cigar to celebrate the birth. If you will look at the label, you will see it says: "Theatre De Lys, eight performances a week. Be advised the actors speak so clearly you need not miss a line."

I I

SINCE IT IS OBVIOUS from the previous part of this introduction that the playwright was in love with his play long before opening night, the question for the second part may be: what does he think of *The Deer Park* now that it breathes on the live and all but bleeding boards, and the quickest answer, madam, is that he broods but a little about his own dear play and thinks often of the life of the theatre.

But, wait! *The Deer Park* opened to a curious set of reviews, mixed in the extreme: "Unearthly depravity," said my old friend, *Time* magazine, kicking us in the ear. "A breath of fresh air," was the manly word from *The Wall Street Journal*. Others cried out we were "passionately comic," "shocking and funny," so forth. Nonetheless, nearly every review was condescending. While it was more or less agreed that for a flamboyant and somewhat over-rated novelist, the apprentice playwright had a modest flair for the theatre, it was also generally regretted that our apprentice included long soliloquies whose sentiments were sophomoric, platitudinous, and presumptively philosophical. (You may now study these soliloquies at your leisure.) It was further considered in meatball taste for him to pop in a speech about the war in Vietnam. That, by consensus, was regarded as an obvious attempt to modernize a ten-year-old play. Since the speech about Vietnam was lifted, however, from the novel and had therefore been written originally in 1951 and 1952 (with the Korean war on the mind), such criticism contained its unwitting ingredient for tonic—besides, excitement in the company was general. We were a hit. Not a smash hit, but a hit. So went the word in New York. When you are a hit, you are a victor. At least, you are running. You do not mind the pricks and darts.

Still the playwright was considerably confused. His play had been helped to keep running by extracting crucial nuggets from in and out reviews, phrases like "sensational," "soars like a skyrocket," "dazzlingly wicked," "endearingly wicked," "scenes which palpitate like the hearts of a couple in the act of love." Properly weeded, we were a full neon garden of fireworks, searchlights, explosions, comedy. "Evil is a fun thing," said Mr. Kerr, putting us down. We nearly put it up.

The theatre is like a marriage—you hate to lose. A marriage which goes down is like a ship which sinks; so is a play. Principles are thrown overboard to keep the living alive. You do not say, "We will shut down *The Deer Park* because there is something disgraceful and deadening to the heart in advertising a play which is serious, as a play which is not." You seize the quotes—ripped, often as not, all bloody from their context—you make do with what you've got. The theatre reserves her awards for those who win. It is liverish to be a loser in the theatre. The play may be a hit for the wrong reasons, but you even feel good. If the reviews have had next to nothing to do with your intent, the illusion of winning is nonetheless sweet, even as staying alive is sweet. Our apprentice, therefore, could afford to be intrigued by the reception of his play. He had a hit on the basis of quoting reviews he could not quite recognize as being related to his own work—they seemed to speak of another play. (Perhaps some work of collaboration by Celine and Saroyan.) Of course he had a production where virtues were mixed with flaws—he knew the values and vices of his actors' performances to a point, or thought he did. He had a large blessing and small curse for every actor in his company and it was a fine company which had shown courage on opening night, all thirteen actors. He had a bit of love for the director, and moments when he could strike him dead. Yet the playwright's soul was in its yaws again. He felt becalmed in a nasty double-edged murmur, as if the hint of a breeze tickled first one ear, then the other, then all sails fluttered. He was annoyed. He felt he had lost his own sure sense of value. He did not know how much he liked his play, nor whether it was really any good. Was it possible that it was only boring, comic, and sensational? And he had nothing by which to measure. He had not seen anything on Broadway in several years. So to keep his critical measure, he went on a tour of the theatrical season and saw more than a dozen plays in two weeks. He was then obviously anxious to learn a little of the nature of the invisible assignation between a drama critic and his favorite girl, a fat smash hit.

But, first he had the good sense to contemplate in advance the differences between book reviewing and theatre reviewing. Doubleday, or Simon & Schuster, or any publishing house which goes by some such name, may spend half a million dollars for a book by Harold Robbins or Irving Wallace, but the novels of these writers will not be reviewed on Page One of the *New York Times* Book Review. The *New York Times* Book Review is guilty of many a crime, but it does not often commit gross hierarchical adulteration. Mr. Robbins may even be put on Page 50. He will certainly hit no better than Page 4. Odds-on he will get a bad or facetious review. And no one except the author will suffer too much. Not even the sales.

But on Broadway! Well, we know what happens to a $500,000 musical. It is a public event more important than the Royal Shakespeare Company doing Shakespeare—the big musical runs equal in glamour and category to the opening of a major new play by Williams or Miller or Albee. And is reviewed not only with the same solemnity, but the same hyperbole. Or more. The critics are often critical of Mr. Williams, but for the book and lyrics, we can write the quotes ourself. "An evening of magical wonder." "An occasion of musical splendor." "A heart-warming, life-giving two hours of uproarious fun." Quick! Give us the name of this musical so that we may see it. But the name, friends, is always *"Our Newest Turd Has Just Moved In."* "Shit, señorita," says Broadway.

Full Stop! All speed astern! Dare the playwright speak thus of *Man of La Mancha* and *Fiddler on the Roof*? Can he include *The Apple Tree* without committing sacrilege? Yes, is the answer, he can—hold all breath. Crimes have been committed in the name of criticism, and the king is damnably naked. *Fiddler on the Roof* is declared a masterpiece when it is next door to a swindle; *Man of La Mancha* is a great creation, except—don't breathe it—there are pits of monotony in the core of its charm. *Apple Tree* is celebrated for introducing a new dimension to musical comedies; in fact it has shoved together a trio of one-act plays, two poor, one good, the total saved by the impressive talents of Barbara Harris.

Well, if our apprentice critic of the drama is not merely on early foot, his thesis would seem to claim the professional reviewer has a double standard which is the reverse of the standard of the book reviewer: that the seriousness of your production—all rare exceptions admitted—is generally measured by the cost of your production. Be it understood the costly production is often a superb production with superb performances (usually by the dancers) but from the playwright's point of view, this is not so different from judging the literary merit of manuscripts by the excellence of the handwriting.

In the two weeks just past, the apprentice playwright saw a great deal of excellent handwriting. He saw *Hello, Dolly!*, and *Barefoot in the Park, Man of La Mancha, The Apple Tree, The Odd Couple, Don't Drink the Water, At the Drop of Another Hat.* He saw *Natural Look, The Homecoming* and *Black Comedy.* He saw—he ran out of plays on Broadway. There was Off-Broadway: *MacBird, Eh?, America Hurrah, Hogan's Goat, The Mad Show.* He saw *The Deer Park* many times. He had evidence in plenty and some new thought to masticate in detail (for what is a critic without his teeth?). Finally, he even had a critical formula. It came from his own work. It explained the mystery of the schizophrenia in the drama reviewer's heart, for the answer was simple: there were two kinds of plays. That was the beginning of what it was all about.

Would you like a metaphor to ease your way? Let the playwright tell a story he heard last night. It is perhaps apocryphal, but not grievously so, for if the story is unfair, you could change the names of the artists until you had a proper fit. This, at any rate, is how the tale was told. Some years ago, William de Kooning gave a drawing to Robert Rauschenberg, who then promptly erased the drawing and signed his own name to the smudged page. Next, the erased drawing was sold. Children, we are not discussing the final absurdity of certain terminal positions in modern art right here, no, sir, we are in on a primitive rite, the writing of money. Primitive man took a stand on a stone. He said, "I am the leader of this tribe, and I stand on this stone, and so this stone has the value of all your tents and all your wives and all your herds and flocks." And since no one was strong enough to kill the leader, the rock on which he stood was money. Before money can be used for barter, it is first declared— it is made into money by an act of declaration. "I, Robert

17

Rauschenberg, hereby make of this piece of paper a piece of money." An erased drawing is restored in value by a signature. Emptiness plus authority equals money.

It seems we are now ready to talk of certain plays, the ones which might put the signature on the erased drawing. They are authority stamped upon emptiness, they are money. The authority of such plays is that they are known as a hit. That is their value. That is how they give value to an audience.

Look at the nightly event. A horde of the hard-working pours in from the suburbs for a night of food and play-going. If they are tired, it is not because they have toted that bale of cotton all day, no, they are tired because their nerves are stale, flat, bored, and unendurable from the stale, flat, unprofitable work they have done as a horde of the middle and professional class all day in offices which buy and sell commodities less interesting and less well-made than they used to be, and they have stifled in modern kitchens and driven children to school and gotten caught in suburban traffic and blinked their eyes against the glare of super shopping-centers. They have rushed and they have waited every day of the week—they have lived lives devoted to controlling their environment—their umbilical relation to existence is now captured in the touch of a fingertip on the plastic button of some electrical machine. They are thus a class which is devoted utterly to control, and they have lost control of everything. If we are to dwell on the Broadway theatre audience and its relation to a hit, we can only talk first of the heart of the theatre—this liberal complacent materialistic greedy pill-ridden anxiety-laden bored miserable and powerless jumble of suburban couples who jam every Broadway smash for the first few months. Later, they are joined, and still later replaced, by tourists, conventioneers, small-towners about to drown in New York, and corporation label-men with the names of the hits to drop back into the office hopper at home. There are out-of-town philosophers buried among the culls of this audience, but out-of-towners in New York are usually using all their wit to dare the subway—they cannot arrive in their seat at their critical best, for they are in

18

New York, Fun City, they want only to be reassured they will not be mugged in the next few hours. So their synapses blend in with all the fear-ridden reflexes of all the liberal couples from the suburbs, and what you get is the middle-class horror of America (and the hint of how Vietnam finally is possible), for our people are in their seats, sprawled out, nervous, vitiated, on the giggle, dying to be manipulated. External manipulation is authority, manipulation heralds the presence of money. But only a hit can manipulate such an audience for they do not wish to contemplate ambiguity—ambiguity is the essence of their nausea and their fatigue. (More of this later.) Listen carefully to such an audience laugh, and you can feel the undertow which attends the manipulation, you may even hear the silent machines which make the money. The Broadway audience being an over-manipulated apathetic flesh stirs only to the intense sound of such silent machines, for those who live in the suburbs are addicted to processes which make money as simply as juvenile delinquents are hipped on marijuana. Addiction, like faith, is focus from a point of reference.

Are we too abstract? Let us take the best of examples for the other side, and think of Zero Mostel, who is curator of a rich large talent. There are many who would say he is a great actor. Some might not agree altogether, but no matter, possessed of moments of grandeur, and moments not so grand, Mostel is nonetheless a major theatrical artist, for he glides like a shark through that medium of mood we might call prime attention in the theatre, his movements slice into the center of a laugh, a roll of his eyes turns a spill of amusement through the aisle. He is a comic wind.

But the evil is this. He does not need to act any more. He can come out on stage, and the audience will laugh. If he scratches his crotch, the house breaks down. If he looks at another actor and merely turns away, the ticket-payers are instantly in delight. Let me whisper the next. If some unknown actor made up to look like Mostel came out for a minute and stood still and scratched his crotch and looked at another actor and looked away, the house might

19

break into equal combers of hysteria provided they did not know it was not Mostel. That collective Broadway flesh wishes only to be manipulated. Mostel rat-tat-tatting his fly is pressing a button to make them laugh. It does not matter whether he is scratching these jewels in *A Funny Thing Happened on the Way to the Forum,* or in *Fiddler on the Roof.* The act of scratching is more important than the play, which is why he is not always a great actor. Audiences laugh because Mostel is the signature on that piece of paper, he is switching on the machines which make the money.

Zero is, of course, an artist of the first rank. When one gets down to the real stuff, however, down to that stretch of hits on Broadway where one ten-dollar bill is the same as the next, when you get all the way down to *Cactus Flower* and talentless technicians of high skill like Barry Nelson, then children, you may be really in the place where the Creation is denied.

There are those who will now suspect a thesis is coming. They may be confident. The thesis is soon to be made by discussing five plays which do not deserve to be discussed separately, for they are not five plays but one play, since their internal mechanisms of manipulation are not individual but collective, and came not out of artists but computers. So specific criticism would have no real bone to bite. (Only a plastic cigar.) Besides, these plays are traitors to the stage: their secret allegiance is to television. When we discuss these plays, we will not be so foolish as to talk of their separate plots, for that would assume the original impulse had been creative rather than computed. Good. These five plays are nominally called *The Odd Couple, Barefoot in the Park, Cactus Flower, Don't Drink the Water,* and *Natural Look.* In fact, by existential measure, they had the duration of only two-and-one-half plays to this reviewer, since he walked out of each one at the end of the first act (which is how first he discovered their common denominator). On such a commencement one might normally have to say no more than that the basic provender of these evenings was watered oatmeal, but months and years ago, the critics had all been in like Flynn, and so the audience responded on each of our nights with a particular barking of laughter which called to mind a human tissue in a Petri dish swaying to calculated shock. A revolutionary with a sawed-off shotgun might in a rage have sprayed the critics hard enough to keep them off their seats because no humanoid tissue could have liked these plays if he had been told they were not to be liked. Subsequently, however, by a work of fierce concentration, compassion for critics was generated by the mind. Drama reviewers, all said, must have been desperately miserable in infancy, and wretched little feeders, to so enjoy watered oatmeal TV, punctuated only by good old Broadway Nursey's running gags (Whoo-hoo, baby, crazy, rattle, crazy). Gruel and gags are sum and substance to infants' bellies. Five pieces of Show Biz—say, nay!—five pieces of Telev Biz—put five bowls of oatmeal down the New York drama critics' collective tummy. Five hits went up. Call it five minus one. Because *Natural Look,* a work as tasteless, empty, skillful, well-acted, and well-directed as the other four is a shade of a hair less satisfactory in hiding the fact that it possesses no fleshly meaning, and so it closes after opening night. Who knows where the styrene will crack? Plastic is a gas in solid form. It can only pretend to flesh.

Strike it like this: *Cactus Flower, Don't Drink the Water, The Odd Couple,* and *Barefoot in the Park* encourage underground spleen because they are The Theatre of Plastic, their content is TV, they are thus cooked of synthetics. Only danger is that the mode by which we perceive reality can indeed become our reality, a most elegant Marxian manner of saying that no medium is more of a message than TV—which may be why, despite the reek of the hot cigar butt, none of us can ignore McLuhan's total slogans. McLuhan has one great grip on the attention of this decade—we all know something in us slides off slowly and begins to die as we watch TV. So the medium is indubitably giving us a message. Feel the message. Salts wash out of your blood, hate and lust pass over to headache. Spook-show in the psyche, cramp in the groin.

21

Love, tenderness, sympathy become vectors to anxious attention. Do not speak of what we see—what we see on TV can be anything—this is talk rather of lobotomizations which seep into the gray collective soul of the room after an evening of TV. Emotions are modulated (rather say: strangled, filtered, choked) while passing through the electronic valves of the transmitter and the set. Something leaves us each night spent in attendance on the box. For the medium has one message—technological society will make certain you pass away on a bed into which national music is piped.

So these Cactus Flowers are not merely bad commercial plays called good plays by the bad taste of the critics, no, they are not even put on the way bad plays used to be, because back, way back then, in return for a definite waste of time, you could still get some raunchy funky little hint of theatre. But, Mr. President, these Cactus Flowers offer preparation for nothing but the sick bed in the last ward. Let me tell you. America has been watching television for twenty years and the style of television has transfused itself not only into the taste, but the demand, even the expectancy, of the suburban middle-class—that precise compound of neurons and suet so capable of being smelted into money. Therefore, Broadway comedies now rush not only to be like television comedies, but actors are trained away from theatre in the process, and sometimes look like television sets come to life. Their emphasis is not to provoke emotion, but to bring you in on reaction, for cool reaction is a good mountain boot going up the game of status.

Television, you see, was the midwife and the child of the now lost Age of Conformity which came to America after the Second World War. (A bad metaphor, but a dream in dialectics—dig, we must.) Television, you may agree, produced a genre: moderate characters in modest situations. (One Woman's Family in a ranch-house.) It offered endlessly recognizable detail, *surface* detail: supermarkets, highways, suburban streets, pastel-colored classrooms. However, the characters in such television dramas presented under microscopic analysis nothing which was finally and

22

biologically real. They bore the same relation to human beings which vinyl does to leather. And the reason was that the characters of these TV series were synthesized from incompatibles—the new documentary and the old soap opera.

Soap opera had a sentimentality which was surrealistic, but its characters—while altogether psychotic—were still real. Since they lived on your radio, their voices came out of a background much like a cave: there was no confusion in one's mind with the here and now of daily surface. The soap opera was material for your dreams. Whereas, catch television. It projects the very latest surface of reality—it goes on hunts for real backgrounds, it is documentarily obsessed. The documentary is, it may hope, its honest buck. Since it then thrusts its own highly sophisticated mutants, (hey, Ginger! hi, Flipper) of the old soap opera characters into highly documentary situations, the dramatic product produces that same vivid sense of displacement from reality you can receive from a painted plaster hamburger by Claes Oldenburg five feet in diameter. You don't know immediately whether the object is comic, nauseating, or significant of some new reality, or even some new way of studying reality. Oldenburg's hamburger is, of course, a way to study a reality which is all before our fingers but for our eyes. But the housewife studying herself on a situation comedy in her electronic mirror does not know if the seemingly recognizable (and therefore sanitizing) characters before her are in their bizarre (and therefore disturbing) situations because they have more wit than herself, or less; she pays for the human pleasure of recognizing some part of herself by a most indigestible psychic demand—she is plunged further into ambiguity (security and anxiety at the same point) and therefore further into obsession with herself. If the old radio soap opera encouraged schizophrenia by offering possible archetypes to every secret desire of the housewife's buried dream and buried secret plot (loyalty to the home vs. hots for the lover) television dulls her into nausea. Fundamental distinctions between the safe and the insecure, the reality and the dream, are marinated, dra-

23

matic oppositions are bypassed—powerful conflicts are first modulated, then mashed into one another. The side effect is nausea.

Superb, you will say, now tell Mr. President why television cannot offer stories and situations which are either frankly disturbing or honestly pacifying, and the answer takes us right back to Marshall Mac. The medium is the message, yes, and a half-hour drama on television cannot be too pacifying or you will notice all too clearly the infernal sound of the set, feel its electronic harp, even—enter op art—see the very vibrations which erode your optic nerve. Yet one cannot go in the other direction: a story must not be too disturbing, for there is no actor's flesh and blood to warm you from a stage, nor, as in a movie, the bodies of the audience, no, you are all alone with your family and the emotional rigors of the tale, plus the psychic assault of the set. Television attacks the unconscious like a trip in a jet—you move from continent to continent or spectacle to spectacle without the accompaniment of a change in mood to prepare the flesh. (The unconscious thus becomes like that poor patient who is operated upon without warning.) So a work of deep drama on television would inspire anxiety, for one's own depths might open to what?—to the baleful electronics of which far off God? what cold star? No, you keep it neat. The scene is recognizable to ward off any shriek, and the situations are odd and out of focus—just sufficiently unsettling to keep your mind off the flickering of the set. Now, you students of existential mechanics, estimate the difficult problems facing our Broadway Computers when they, hung on the firm premise that all sound commercial theatre must be based on television tales (because audiences are now based on the narrative synapses of the television series), are next obliged to translate or computerize the technique from one medium to another. (Come, McLuhan, you have not enough to say on this.) Yeah. You now have real actors forced to imitate actors as they appear to us, no, rather as they impact our nerves, from a television set. You must have backgrounds which are recognizable, but situations which do not exist, you must reconstruct in the

24

audience that hum of security and insecurity which is a television set. Since you have real actors who can be generally depended upon to give the audience a moment of true warmth at the end (since that is finally what the actors are for), the psychic payoff on all Cactus Flowers is huge—it is like watching television with a homecooked meal at the end. The only one who can suffer in these plays is the actor, for he is thrust into a cancerous relation with his art—too much approbation too little deserved must flux his guilt, and skillful emotion skillfully applied to a situation which does not exist in the blood of his past experience must be as conducive to leukemia as kissing a plastic mask on the hour.

The medium is the message, and the message of television is electronic hum. The theatre will wash down from its old broken-down heights to the swamps of TV, the theatre—if it continues, as it will, to cohabit with TV, —is close to an excruciating death by long wallowing, for the smelting operations will enlarge, and the big houses will continue to be filled with armies of pill-fed humanoids in for the night from television. The Theatre of Manipulation will swell in every joint. It will thrive like edema. And the critics will be the doctors who call this swelling, health. For it is true. To talk of Broadway is to talk not of amusement but disease.

Yes, it seems that no less a task is before us than to forgive all drama critics for invariably amputating the wrong organ—but then they are blind and ill themselves. Have pity on them. They are men who fell in love early with illusion and so cannot leave now that the lady has become an electronic ghost. Drama critics cannot see themselves as necrophiliacs. They must believe that TV's Theatre of Manipulation: watered surrealism and pistol shot gags, is still the butler to art, not its avenging ghost.

And is that all to be said for the season? These five plays which are one play and lead to no discussion of the stage, only polemics and existential analyses of the evils of television? The answer is: bring on the band and certainly not! The apprentice put in two weeks going to shows, and he is not likely to let anyone away without a capsule of comment for each evening. Besides, one would not wish the rest of Broadway to escape the brute—let him tamp in a bruise or two. Here. Listen to more about *Man of La Mancha* and *Fiddler on the Roof,* stay close and you will pick up criticism—we whisper it—of *Black Comedy,* exactly where it crosses *At the Drop of Another Hat.* But first, Mr. President, we must interrupt with a commercial, a word on the problem from my own play. Witness! A director and a producer exchange dialogue:

MUNSHIN

Extraordinary.

EITEL

You really like it?

MUNSHIN

It's an epic study about the hole in eternity our country is preparing for itself. It's a poem. This can make the greatest picture in the last ten years.

EITEL

Collie, why don't you say what you really think?

MUNSHIN

(Fingering his belly)
No audience would understand it.

EITEL

I think it would be amazing how much this would communicate to an audience.

MUNSHIN

You don't communicate with an audience, you manipulate an audience . . .

The producer is an old-fashioned producer. His type went out ten years ago. Producers are not so full of energy any more, and they study audiences with the aid of motivational research and statistics on consensus. Mr. Munshin had a simpler idea. To manipulate an audience you put on a rubber glove (although he did not need a rubber glove) and you put your finger up as far as it would

26

go. Pop! That was the old-fashioned movie and the old-fashioned smash Broadway success. Well, history is composed of layers—one is not the first to suggest it. So talk of TV's Theatre of Manipulation must not be confused with good old Collie Munshin's plumber's snake of a finger. No, Collie was brought up on Zing, went the strings of my heart—emotional sap must be there to keep Collie happy. The old Collie Munshin Theatre of Manipulation depended not on thin emotionless mismarriages between surrealism and the documentary, but on *schmaltz, shtick* and Collie's finger maneuvering up the seat of all critical opposition.

Well, it sours the face to say this, but one can get so pleased with the fact that this abysmal old theatre of corned manipulation is not dead, that the sins of *Fiddler on the Roof* and *Man of La Mancha* could kindly be forgiven, if lunar hyperbole had not been attached to them.

But, hear! *Fiddler on the Roof* may not be the greatest musical ever made. In fact, it may be never nearly so good as *Pal Joey*. Listen to your favorite brute. Let us enjoy an excursion into literary affairs. If Sholom Aleichem was almost a great writer, his particular weakness was—go through the work—a determined inability to confront evil in intimate forms—he preferred to present evil as some external abstract force—a catastrophe, a pogrom, a drunken peasant. With such a view, one is always close to the danger of the over-sentimental. (Look! That good man got killed for nothing.) *Fiddler on the Roof* (adaptation from a book by Maurice Samuel, *The World of Sholom Aleichem*) has added Samuel's own pervading sentimentality to Aleichem's sweet wit, and the result—surprisingly tuneless—is a hard all-out Munshin-ish manipulation of Jewish audiences, for *Fiddler* plays with no quarter on emotions of self-righteousness, self-pity, ignorance, and guilt. In fact, guilt should well be mentioned first—it is so obviously felt by the audiences for that past they have evaded (no, let us say they have jettisoned) in the race to the suburb, it is the blood guilt of all the prayers which have not been said, and all the stones which have not been laid on all the graves of all the grandparents. The audience

27

is milked like a cow, but the loss of milk feels sweet to them, for these suburbanites know next to nothing of life in the *shtetl*—it is all revelation to them—they are pleased to discover their own past is nearly so colorful as the old country life of Sicilians and Bavarians and Ukrainians. Yes, indeed, *shtetl* life is indeed colorful as presented in *Fiddler on the Roof*—but not very much more accurate, says the brute, than a musical about peasants and gypsies by MGM.

Man of La Mancha is a more exciting play and so commits a greater sin, for it manipulates one of the deepest desires of us all—which is to be noble. It plays with the joy of fulfilling this dream, and the agony of losing it. So it moves audiences to tears. But it is only a good play, and work on such a theme begs to be great. *La Mancha*'s music is thin when arias might be near, and its language is undernourished. It does not inhabit the high desires nor fill the dungeons of the emotional architecture to which it pretends. It merely gives a hint of a spark and lets the audience blow it into fire with the gale of that most curious hunger—to be noble, to be true to one's dream. But the play is not true to the demand of the theme—rather it is clever enough to see that the time has come to send Jeanette MacDonald and Nelson Eddy to college. Survey of World Literature I—let's go Don Quixote!

Let us rather make a terrible confession, for that is a way to arrive at the point with a minimum of ballast and all sails high—the brute liked *Hello, Dolly!*. He liked it better than *Man of La Mancha* and *Fiddler on the Roof*. It was in fact likable because it was too crude to manipulate even a ten-year-old. It had only its own gusto to offer, and the best music of all the shows, and the best dancing. So it was good the way a ball club is good. Therefore, it only expressed one aspect of the theatre, one-half of the theatre, but that half it expressed altogether—that mindless half which speaks of physical health, sex, top bananas, and bazazz. Besides, it had Ginger Rogers giving what may have been the best performance ever she gave on the night the apprentice critic saw it, she did everything with a kind

28

of stomp-it-out kick-it-up vitality, and the love of birthday cakes was in her eye, she had the rare beauty of the plump blonde when the blonde is concupiscent, and at the end she received bravos like a bullfighter and deserved them. And even gave a curtain speech with happy smiles and generous tears. A noisy evening ended in theatrical rainbows of love. The theatre can get away with anything when it makes a rainbow.

The theatre can also get away with anything when it is sufficiently surgical to make a brilliant incision into the nature of reality, or of desire, and do that in pure theatrical context. Witness the vast success respectively of *Black Comedy* and *At the Drop of Another Hat*. *Black Comedy* cuts right into the phenomenology of the real. It points out that if you encounter a hot hot-dog and roll in the dark, your hand will fly away as if it had encountered a turd, a dog's muzzle, or a hot set of tools. Now turn the light up for the audience, but let the actors pretend they are in the dark. Yes, we have sudden and brilliant incision into the nature of reality. Study those actors, ho! One laughs for the first twenty minutes and then waits for the moment when the play will step out to explore its premise. But *Black Comedy* has got the playwright's hand on the silent machine which makes the money and so it refuses resolutely to explore its own magic. Instead, it rushes to cash in its profits. Like a truly nasty upper-class London accent, it goes in for a witless repetitive obsessive strangling of the premise. It explores no more. Our audience having been exercised first to laugh, is then extorted to laugh, finally is tortured and at last debauched by laughs which are by now become no more than conditioned reflexes, and therefore leave the psyche as quiet and empty as the theatre ten minutes after final curtain. When the English loot a bank, they even get the pennies which roll under the carpet.

In line with this sort of robbery, absolute thoroughness is indispensable, and Flanders and Swann, our next protagonists, are thorough—they mine every aspect of the muted desire to share in theatre which characterizes their most special sort of audience. The brute could say that *At*

29

the Drop of Another Hat is prime pigeon feed for Wasps, for they are the most underfed patrons of the theatre, and he would be right. *At the Drop of Another Hat* is resolutely non-nasty, and keen as calling cards. It suggests in its assortment of songs and anecdotes (funny little ditties about the need of others to be obscene, extracts from Tolkien, etc.) the buried and doubtless not altogether bona fide memory of the best and wittiest visits of a fine British clergyman and his sexton on Sunday afternoons in June in golden British gardens there in the quiet twilight of the empire—nothing can move the heart of a Yankee banker more. *At the Drop* is indeed so resolutely non-nasty that one senses through the whirring of the pigeon's wings that the real ugliness of the proceedings is buried in the profoundly admiring complacency of audience and performers for each other as they swell their breasts back and forth, mourning secretly for the power of empire they think has been lost, when in fact, it is the same people ultimately who fly the planes and burn the babies.

Which brings us to psychosis, the second most crowded pathology in American life. (Do not deaden the proceedings by mentioning the first.) In addition to *Hello, Dolly!*, there were five plays for which the brute had good words, and four of them had to do with madness, and only one, *Mac-Bird,* was, with that, content—the three others, *America Hurrah, The Mad Show* and *The Homecoming* pushed on into the most modern movements and logics of madness, on to the most advanced field of psychosis which seems composed of a total all-but-hermetic surface across which lies a thundering crack. Yet no one can find this abyss. So these three plays explored the anxiety of living on a plane and looking for a void, and because they were deeply conceived, they had no impulse to manipulate, no, rather there was some depth of mood they wished to achieve by working up the details of an obscure magic between the audience and themselves. Therefore the plays roused a presence which was like a monster or a machine or a beast. (In *The Mad Show* it was a sad sweet humor about the eye of the wacky.) But in the two others the beast lived on the stage and shared your horror and so permitted laughter, and moments occurred in *The Homecoming* and *America Hurrah* where one was in the presence of that mysterious communion of mood which can be experienced nowhere but in the theatre.

This sense of a presence was achieved in *The Homecoming* through a quiet modest exhibition of the propinquity of the common place and the psychotic. Its glint of genius was to demonstrate the thesis by showing what exactly was equal to what. Each character recounting the dullest details of his day was equal to the casual attention of a family group as they watched a wife and brother-in-law roll on the floor in embrace. So it was perhaps a play which was talking about the end of any world we know or perhaps it was like a street one passes in a dream, and on this street a murder is committed. In your dream. In its turn, *America Hurrah* went through sometimes tedious, if always intelligent, insights into the maniacal surface of all programmed communications, and then exploded at the end with ten minutes that lived on the edge of the lip of the murder of all American life and the carnage of the psyche, and the death of the American vision.

Then, there was *MacBird*. *MacBird* had a truth for which the apprentice was not prepared. Beneath the parody was a wild sorrow, for suspicion flooded the heart that LBJ had more real life as MacBird than as Lyndon Johnson—one could conceive of him secretly watching MacBird with tears in his eyes: the role and the language gave him a stature life had denied.

This would be a fair quick summation of the plays one saw, and the lessons learned, and the coldest lesson came from the best plays—the future of the theatre seemed most rich where the material was most insane. A cold note. Therefore, *Hogan's Goat* was reserved for comment last, since it is out of category. A passionate and substantial work overwritten by a degree, it had another kind of sorrow, for it displayed the blood beneath the corruption and gave a feel of the muscle within the piety of the Irish in Brooklyn, New York, some generations back and that was no modest achievement.

Do you get the point? Good plays like *The Homecoming*,

31

MacBird, America Hurrah, The Mad Show, Hogan's Goat
(and you know the other) are plays which attempt to find
a piece of that most mysterious and magical communion
some call ceremony, some church, and some theatre. They
are plays which attempt to reach a moment sufficiently
magical to live in the deepest nerves and most buried
caves of the memory of the people who have seen them,
these plays speak of the fire at the edge of the wood and
hair rising on the back of the neck when the wind becomes
too intimate in its sound. The theatre lives (if it lives as anything more than a spinster aunt on allowance from movies,
television, and the record business), the theatre lives on
what it can do uniquely, on moods of depth and perfume
and terror and exaltation and cascades of laughter which
no other form can provide—it is a ceremony which takes
place in a cave, and philosophers, priests, painters, tyrants,
and athletes must collaborate, the bodies of some must
harmonize with the minds of others. When it is really good,
what it offers can be found in no other form of art, for
then it is like religion for the irreligious and gives promise
of something which may live forever. Its impermanence is
the life of its power. But that is only true of those finest
plays which never manipulate, and there are not so many.
This year on Broadway the number is down to two or
one, this real species of theatre has about given way to all
the hybrid giants in the palaces on Broadway, those Cactus
Flowers whose sins against the loving heart of the Lord
are performed at the rate of a thousand a minute, for a
thousand humanoid hearts are laughing at jokes which
were conceived in the same place they used to package
thalidomide and will package the actors tomorrow when
the actors perform the benefits for themselves in the camps
of concentration. "Shit, señorita," says Broadway.

A NOTE ON THE PRODUCTION

THE PLAY CAN BE STAGED in the round or on a conventional stage, but in either case the attempt must be made to suggest that the set bears some relation to the inner space of Sergius O'Shaugnessy's memory, that the audience is in effect living within his mind. So the play could be staged happily in a tent.

But, observe! Since the action unrolls in memory, the set may with a minimum of furnishings and props symbolize a variety of rooms and places. It will be by turns the ranch home of Charles Francis Eitel, the patio of Dorothea O'Faye's home, a nightclub, Marion Faye's home, Lulu Meyers' hotel room, the town of Desert D'Or itself. Props, for example, are at a minimum and should suggest rather than declare themselves. With the exception of Sergius, who drinks a visible fluid the color of whiskey throughout the play, all other actors will drink imaginary coffee from real cups, sip at imaginary drinks poured from real but empty decanters into visible but empty glasses.

But in fact there is no need to define where each event takes place, or even precisely how it takes place. Remembered conversations do not always occur in a concrete and clearly recollected environment; imagination creates conversations which never existed anywhere but in the illumination of the mind. So the scenes of *The Deer Park*, here called "Changes," are for the most part numerous and brief and take place in shafts of light, in spotlights,

33

before searchlights, in sudden bright lights, in dim lights. There is no attempt made to show where a particular scene is taking place—that will take care of itself for the action will usually define the location, and where it does not, no matter, the action is finally within the recollection and imagination of the narrator, in those aisles and caverns, those metaphorical forests and desert of the mind. Since the mind most often moves quickly, the action most often must be quick. Furniture is not to be taken off and on between scenes (a further reason for it to be kept at a minimum) and indeed one omnibus piece consisting of desk, couch, bed and bench, all in one, can serve promiscuously as a central focus for the action in any scene which suggests a room. The design of this omnibus may even excite the ingenuity of the set designer. (Indeed there is almost no other solution for staging *The Deer Park* in a small place.) On a larger stage, enclaves of action defined by overhead lights and one or two small fixed pieces of furniture sitting perhaps on a low platform may be used to suggest Eitel's home, Faye's home, Teppis' thròne, and so forth. These enclaves will be respected as *querencias* —actors will not enter them witlessly. For instance, during the set of scenes or Changes which take place at Dorothea O'Faye's party, the entire stage will serve as a sort of patio, and action will flow around these enclaves, but it will not flow through them. Those small defined empty areas will serve to remind the audience of actions which have already taken place, even as an old coat may remind us of last year's love.

Two further elements are suggested for the staging. The play is about Hollywood as well, not the Hollywood of the Twenties, the Thirties, the War Years, the blacklists of the Fifties, the pills, the socialized orgies and the television studios of the Sixties, but rather it is about all these Hollywoods as they coalesce in the amalgam of memory; so the play does not take place in one time or in one particular year, but rather occurs in some undefined time after the Second World War and offers us echoes of all the decades, for even the Hollywood of the silent film lives in the memory and experience of many of the characters, it has

34

shaped their characters and given them some of the precise details of their personal style. For that reason, since this is so completely a play about Hollywood which takes place in an imaginary town called Desert D'Or (not necessarily unrelated to that motel spa, Palm Springs) one does well in presenting the play to give some hint of a sound stage. The overhead lights, the frenels and lekos and dinkies will work to purpose, and their cables may be exposed, even hang down into the audience in extreme circumstances. Two searchlights small in scale but similar in style to the great columnar lights of the film premiers could be used to advantage before the play and during the intermission. A moving spotlight could be used to follow the movements of the actors in certain scenes. Needless to say this cinematographic note must not dominate the production. The play takes place in memory—so much of its playing must be resonant, evocative of mood, sensuous, the way memory is sensuous. (Note: Sensuous, not sensual, or oversexed. The last is fatal to a fine production of *The Deer Park* unless done with consummate taste—one does not find consummate taste when ten to twelve actors walk a stage. Not often!) Yes, the play should be, in the best sense, tender— these characters, vain, silly, half-mad with delusion, or mad with Faustian vision, marooned forever from a clear sense of the real, exist nonetheless with pain in their hearts, the pain of lovers, their hearts bleed internally; they live with sorrow. So the glare of the lights and the cables, and the bare electronic canyons of the film process are best suggested now and again, and should not dominate the fact that the play moves through the mind of Sergius O'Shaugnessy and he is full of love by the end, the sort of love which comes not so unexpectedly from understanding the lives of others and forgiving them, even gaining a glimmer of the "true joy of the flesh—rare as the eye of the rarest tear of compassion." Yes, that is the final tone of the play, and the staging must not drown it with tricks, rather it must accent the tenderness and the sorrow, even as salt picks forth the sweetness in melon.

That said, contemplate the trick which is the deepest and most dangerous of all. The play takes place for the

35

most part in quick bits, fragments of scenes and scenelets. They are called "Changes," and suggest the rapid cuts of a film, and there are many of them, even so many as forty-four in the First Act and in the Second. So it is suggested that there be an electric board mounted overhead able to be seen by all, similar to the sort of counter one sees in stadiums or fight clubs or at basketball games where the 24-second rule is dramatized by an electric scoreboard which goes down from 24 to 1 in 24 seconds. So here in the play the changes will each be numbered and will move in the First Act, for example, from Change Forty-four to Change Forty-three all the way down to Change One, the last change of the act. In the Second Act, the numbers will be up again, and again will go down to One. And those scenes which are longer, more important, capture the attention of the director, or need an accent, may be bolstered with supplementary legends under the lights, like "Bet the Red," or "Double Your Money on Red," or "Wait for Seven," and such changes should appear in red lights when they come up rather than in white. This, one would repeat, is a dangerous trick—a delicate scene proceeds on stage and overhead is its electric number in white light or red light, and yet managed in such a way as not to dominate the production. This use of numbers is essential to the fun of the evening and the depth of the statement, for we are in effect enjoying a count-down, our anticipations are aroused, our sense of climax is accelerated, and the oppressive sense of a world of atom bombs, Las Vegas, and the fevered electric heart of America's night is never altogether absent as indeed it should not be, for Las Vegas and the apocalyptic sense of the bomb are Hollywood's children, yes both, a remark whose truth may be sensed long before it can be proved. But indeed the theatre has little need of proof. Evocation is its heaven, boredom is its hell—any man so mad and fine-inspired as to attempt to direct this play of *The Deer Park* will know his efforts have failed unless the audience, speechless at the end and too sweetly bruised to applaud, may murmur only, "Heaven, sheer heaven." Of such stuff are playwright's dreams.

COMMENTS ON THE CHARACTERS

Sergius O'Shaugnessy: An Ex-Air Force Flyer on the Loose. (23 or 24) He is the narrator of the play. A tall, well-built young man. Is cocky with an undertone of sadness, and a constant hint of humor. Wry, tough, but always intelligent—which is to say he does his best to conceal the quality of his intelligence.

Marion Faye: A Pimp. (24) Medium in height or under, very special, slim, tight-knit, beautiful, as angelic in appearance as a choirboy, but moves like a quick animal and is possessed of a fine voice, which is by turns rough-edged, musical, incisive, or sadistic as a whip. His presence is intense. He has an arrogance which is made up of staring at you, measuring your value, and deciding you are not there.

Bobby: A Call Girl. (22) Sweet, not too bright, vulnerable, a little brain with quick calculations. A tendency to girlish sighs. A wan, demure expression; a cheerful, valiant, phony tone. She has been taught an actress must use her personality, so she is forever using it, forcing her voice into artificial enthusiasm, artificial disgust, artificial gaiety.

Lulu Meyers: A Movie Star. (25) A little turned-up nose, a dimpled chin, a pouting mouth. Cuddling, curving motions. She seems to bounce when she walks, her shoulders sway in a little rhythm with her hips, her neck curves, her hair falls in a golden sheath, and her husky voice laughs at everyone's jokes. A child-woman, a mistress, a bitch, an absolute narcissist, and most profoundly an actress. Her life is most real when she is acting.

Charles Francis Eitel: A Movie Director. (40 to 55) A man neither handsome nor ugly, but strikingly attractive. His smile is more than normally engaging and his voice is rich in subtle accents—New York is in it, and the theatre, a trace of the South, a hint of the fashionable—it is a voice which varies its style to accommodate the person to whom he speaks, he communicates a sensitive, even fastidious sense of a man playing a scene to some private audience in his mind. So his manner has a way of offering some promise and then pulling it back; the moment you decide he's laughing at you, he seems to like you—about the time you expect things are going well, his voice will turn you away. If his sophistication is always evident, the facets of his nature are revealed by degrees—cynical, sly, idealistic, romantic, noble, corrupt, visionary, strong, weak, tortured, tender, a lover finally.

Carlyle Munshin: A Producer. (40 to 45) Has a broad heartiness. His voice is an appurtenance, it booms, it bleats, it whines, it shouts, it attacks, it groans, it runs away, and all the while he is hiding behind it shrewdly estimating his next move.

Herman Teppis: Head of Supreme Pictures. (in his sixties) A florid man, with a powerful and overpowering manner, sly, sad, incisive, brutal, mean and farcical by turns. An amateur philosopher whose compulsion is to philosophize in every remark. A man utterly in love with his own voice.

Elena Esposito: A Dancer. (25) She is a near-beauty, but this is misleading, for she is not so much beautiful as sexual. She moves in a vale of deep sexual musk. Yet her manner is awkward, vulnerable by striking starts, and a good bit rough. It will take years to finish her. Her voice is thus not one of her assets. By times rich and musical, it also reveals the snarls, the whines, the nasalities, and the sneers of a poor and cruel childhood. Her basic stance is to be wary and sullen, but this is a depression designed to hold together the furious contradictions of her nature; for she is murderous and suicidal, loyal and treacherous, devoted and savage, uneducated, but sensitive, stupid, but lightning shrewd, brave, but timid, cheap finally, and yet in search of an honesty other women might choose to ignore.

Teddy Pope: A Movie Star. (30) Tall, slim, handsome, athletic in appearance, but not rugged—the build of a good tennis player. Probably blue-eyed and blond. Until he begins to camp, there is no particular reason to suppose he is homosexual.

Tony Tanner: Young Actor on the Rise. (25) Big, muscular, vain, animal—patterns himself after the early Brando, but does not quite capture his scene—shows a crudeness Brando managed to avoid.

Dorothea O'Faye: A Gossip Columnist. (early 40's) Handsome woman with a full body, notorious as a showgirl years ago, famous in her nightclub days as a singer. Her boast is that she has been everywhere, has done everything, knows everything there is to know. Rough wit. Forceful style. Brutal but classy. She is Marion Faye's mother.

Don Beda: A Millionaire. (45) Top echelon of the jet set. Beda is tall, distinguished, a goatee, speaks in a slight foreign accent, which could be French, Spanish, Italian, or South American. He is famous in the un-

39

derground history of the fashionable world for his orgies. His charm should suggest the magnificence of someone who pursues the moment with all magical intensity, for one step behind is total boredom.

Zenlia: Beda's Wife. (somewhere in her twenties) She is tall, slender, with platinum silver hair, and a delicate, even exquisite beauty. Speaks in a complete English accent. Her manner betrays the distance, even the island-like isolation of a famous model forever lost in a castle of mirrors which contemplate her loveliness.

NOTE: *The age of the characters may be difficult to fulfill. It is not easy to get young actors to play Sergius, Lulu, Marion, or Elena, since if they have had sufficient experience to understand the role, they have thereby lacked training as an actor, for such experience is opposed to the discipline of schooling. It is suggested therefore that one employ older actors if necessary—the discrepancy in age may be accounted for by Sergius, who could say: (See Page 45—after ". . . sometimes our memory") "But memory is willful. I cannot control the images it offers. People I knew when they were twenty or more are thirty now and thirty-five. They have aged in my mind. Not all, but some. My memory is like a tent which collapses here and pokes up there."*

ACT ONE

PROLOGUE

(From the wing of the theatre, Sergius O'Shaugnessy walks out and stands before the audience. He is dressed in a First Lieutenant's Air Force uniform. In one hand he holds a fifth. As he looks about, he takes a belt of whiskey, and wipes his mouth with the back of his hand. A spotlight is on him.)

SERGIUS

Good evening. My part in what you are about to see is unimportant, yet by another measure I suppose I am very important, even essential. For everything you see here tonight takes place in my mind. Assume we are going then on a little excursion on an underground river of whiskey.

(A nip from the bottle)

Yes, this may be the best opportunity I have to talk about myself,

43

and I admit I feel like talking. There's an unmistakable feeling of nourishment you get from talking to people with real faces. You see, I am not alive.

(Another belt from the bottle)

At least I am not alive as most of you would understand it. Something happened to me while flying an airplane which dropped fire bombs on Orientals. Since I burned more than a few to cinder and enjoyed myself in the act, I was sent here,

(Indicates the set behind him)

here, to this mysterious dimension of moral consequence which most of you call Hell. And here I have remained. But I believe I may not be here forever, because I know where I am. I know that one life ended for me and something else began. This distinguishes me. The men and women you are about to meet believe they are alive. They think they are enjoying themselves in a resort in Southern California. Of course, some of them may guess that if they are a little better than is expected of them, they can return to your side of the footlights. Maybe that is the reason some of us are so moral in our immoral way.

(Another belt from the bottle)

Yes, before you stands a young man who evidently likes to drink. But then a man must drink until he locates the truth, which means,

44

I suppose, that I am a little out of balance. So I suppose are most of you. For we are all obsessed with reality; we wonder what it is. Reality is real only at moments. Yet what vitality persists in the fragments. How real they are—even when they are not necessarily real. Our imagination of what happened to other people becomes sometimes our memory.

(A dance, suggestive of the life of the court at Versailles, strikes up as he continues. The actors enter to the lilts of this dance, some from the wings, some from the rear of the theatre and remain through the prologue.)

So accept me as your guide on a tour through strong sunlight, deep nights, hey hey! and conversations about movies, money and love— love, that roller coaster! The tour begins!

(The actors are seated)

In the cactus wild of Southern California, a distance of two hundred miles from the capital of cinema, is the town of Desert D'Or. It is the only place I know which is all new.

(Lights play about the theatre as if to suggest that the area comprised by the cast and audience is the town itself. Perhaps the cold shriek of an eagle should be heard—the scream of brakes.)

45

I dropped into the resort with fourteen thousand dollars, a sum I picked up in a poker game in a Tokyo hotel room while waiting with other fliers for our plane home. Let me leave it at that. It is the way I remember it. I came out of the Air Force with no place to go, no family to visit, and wandered down here, here to Desert D'Or.

(A third belt from the bottle)

Here—

(The sound is hollow, haunted by reverberations in some tomb of his psyche.)

I got to know a few people.

(Sounds of laughter and ice cubes in glasses)

For instance—I came to see a lot of a highly developed and most mysterious character named Marion Faye.

(Spot on Marion)

He fascinated me. That's the truth.

MARION

How many planes did you shoot down?

SERGIUS

Just three.

MARION

Just three? They lost money on you. You'd have shot down more if you could.

SERGIUS

I would have tried.

46

MARION

You dig killing Asiatics?

SERGIUS

I didn't mean it that way.

MARION

They know how to train you characters. I wasn't an officer.
I went into the Army a private and I came out that way.
I'm the only private they ever had.

SERGIUS

They kept booking you in the stockade, I hear.

MARION

Yes, I learned a thing or two. You see, it's easy to kill a
man. Easier to do that than chase after a roach and
squash it.

SERGIUS

Where do you end up with this?

MARION

I don't know. I got to work it out.

SERGIUS

Faye was a businessman. His operations were modest. He dabbled in
handicrafts.

BOBBY

Marion, I'm sorry, I had to see you.

MARION

Charmed.

BOBBY

It was so extraordinary and unexpected . . .

MARION

I thought I told you never to visit me after three.

BOBBY

Marion, our mutual friend gave me five hundred dollars.

47

MARION

Congratulations.

BOBBY

It was a wonderful night, Marion.

MARION

Sure, you made five hundred.

BOBBY

Oh, it wasn't that. He was so nice to me. He called it a loan. Do you know, Marion, if I ever hit it, I'm going to pay him back.

MARION

Say, it must have gone well.

BOBBY

What a trip.

MARION

Yes, Eitel's got a lot of technique.

BOBBY

It wasn't technique. I think Charley has a crush on me.

MARION

You don't know how sweet he is.
He's a sweet guy.

BOBBY

It was so funny when he saw the kids. Veila woke up and began to cry and he held her and rocked her. I could swear there were tears in his eyes.

MARION

This is before he paid you?

BOBBY

Yes.

MARION

Well, what do you know?

48

BOBBY

You're not being nice. You don't understand. I had the blues today. I was thinking that maybe I couldn't make it sensationally for this kind of work, and Charley Eitel gave me a terrific type lift. He makes you feel like you're something.

MARION

Five hundred. Figuring it one-third to me, two-thirds to you, you owe me one hundred and sixty-six and toodle-dee-oo. I can make change.

BOBBY

Marion, I thought I only owed you seventeen dollars. After all, he was supposed to leave just fifty dollars, wasn't he?

MARION

One-third, two-thirds. That's how it's done.

BOBBY

But I didn't have to tell you how much he gave me. You're penalizing me for being honest.

MARION

Baby, you felt like shooting your mouth off. That's what you're paying me for. Vanity. It's all vanity. I have vanity that I want to be paid.

BOBBY

Marion, you don't know what the extra money means for my children.

MARION

Look, you can go and drown them. That's *all right* with me.

> (*This is said with such quiet author-
> ity that we can see the children
> about to drown*)

BOBBY

Marion, I feel as if there's something I ought to tell you.

49

MARION

Why don't you stop announcing everything you have to say?

BOBBY

Marion, I don't think I'm made out to be a party girl.

MARION

Sure you are. I never met the chick who wasn't.

BOBBY

I was thinking that if it takes with Charley Eitel and myself, well, what I would like is to leave this and all this work as being just a little episode when I was on the rocks. I mean, think of the kids.

MARION

You think Eitel has a hurt for you?

BOBBY

I'm sure he does. He couldn't have acted that way otherwise.

MARION

But he didn't say when he'd see you again.

BOBBY

Well, he didn't say exactly but the way he smiled when he left, I just know that it's going to be soon.

MARION

Let's find out.

(He reaches for the phone)

BOBBY

You're not going to call him now?

MARION

He won't mind getting up. He'll just take another sleeping pill.

EITEL
(At this moment he is not visible; indeed he is no more than a voice on a telephone)

50

Hello.

Charley, it's Faye. I hope I didn't disturb you.

(Bobby snuggles next to Faye to hear)

EITEL
No, no, it's all right. What's it about?

MARION
I'm talking about a date of yours named Bobby. You remember Bobby?

EITEL
Yes, of course.

MARION
Well, I mean like she just left here and she was talking about you. Charley, I don't know what you got, but Bobby digs you. Man, she really digs you.

EITEL
She does?

MARION
Now look, Charley, try and concentrate 'cause I have to make arrangements. When would you like to see Bobby? Tomorrow night? Night after?

EITEL
Oh, God, never.

MARION
Well, thanks, Charley. I'll get you a different kind of chick next time. Beddy-Bye.

(Hangs up)

BOBBY
He was asleep. He didn't know what he was saying.

MARION
I'll call him again.

BOBBY

Marion, that wasn't fair.

MARION

Sure it was fair. Did you ever hear of the unconscious? That's what he was talking from.

BOBBY

He meant the things he said when he was with me.

> *(The lights fade on Marion—we see him left with an angelic smile of pure evil—or is it the evil grin of an angel?)*

> **SERGIUS**

> For a short time here in Desert D'Or, I had something nice going with a girl named Lulu Meyers. Lulu was a movie star.

> *(Spot on Lulu—or grand entrance)*

> I was happy at the thought that one hundred million red-blooded American men must be hating my guts.

LULU

Sugar, I tried and I couldn't make doo-doo. Isn't it awful? What should I eat?

> *(Blackout)*

> **SERGIUS**

> Lulu was a creature. She had nine little women in her.

> *(Spotlight on Lulu)*

LULU

Oh, it's awful! It's awful. When I get older, my breasts are going to droop. There's no way I can stop it. Will you promise to be careful when you touch them, sugar?

SERGIUS

What's the matter?

LULU

Nothing's the matter.

SERGIUS

Something must be the matter. Tell me.

LULU

Oh sugar, it's just that I've always planned to have my breasts raised once they began to sag. Well, I went to see Dorothea yesterday. You know she had that operation.

SERGIUS

No, I didn't know.

LULU

Well, she did—Sugar, they're so unattractive. They're square.

SERGIUS

They aren't.

LULU

But they are. She showed me. They're square. I feel like it's happening to me.

(Blackout)

SERGIUS

Once upon a time, Lulu had been married to a famous movie director—Charles Francis Eitel. A famous movie director, why he was a notorious movie director. Warrior, brawler, movie-maker, night rider of the gossip columns, he was said to have been the cause of more than one million-dollar divorce. Of course, in his turn he had been through three marriages, of which my little Lulu was the last.

53

SERGIUS
(To Eitel)

I met Lulu a couple of nights ago. What with one thing and another we didn't say good-bye until it was time for breakfast.

EITEL

Congratulations.

SERGIUS

You don't mind? I hope you're not jealous.

EITEL

I don't feel a thing. But who knows? I could be dying inside.

(Blackout)

SERGIUS

Still, his films made money and for a time he was the highest-paid director at the studio. He had the reputation of being able to get relatively superlative performances from relatively untalented actresses.

(Spotlight on Lulu holding an Academy Award, giving tears and kisses to the audience)

EITEL

Audiences are composed of sentimental necrophiles. They dine on organs, nectar and blood. And drink pious sentiments. I am the merchant of cowballs and horsepiss.

SERGIUS

Suddenly, three films were failures. He never completed his last picture. In the middle he walked off the set. Then one day his name appeared on a list. He had a dialogue with a legislator. It went like this.

54

SERGIUS
(Playing the part of Crane)
"Patriotism is for pigs." Eitel, do you remember saying that?

EITEL
Senator Crane, I would have put it differently if I had known some agent of your Committee was reporting what I said at a party.

SERGIUS
(As Crane)
How would you put it today?

EITEL
If you ask me to go on, I'll make a subversive remark.

SERGIUS
(As Crane)
I order you to go on. Just how and in what language would you word it for the Committee today?

EITEL
I'd say that patriotism asks you to be ready to leave your wife at a moment's notice. Just possibly that's the secret of its appeal.

(Blackout on Eitel)

SERGIUS
He was then, you see, busted in a marijuana raid. It happened to be only the fifth time in his life he had smoked marijuana but it was a formidable scandal, and he made mistakes with the judge. Contempt of court, jail for two years. He and Marion Faye attended the same campus. They were not cellmates but neighbors.

MARION
If you're curious, I was in for smashing a sports car without a license. Plus one other item. There was a frail in the

car with me who got hurt weird to fear. I was in, you may dig, for beauty slaughter.

> SERGIUS
>
> When Eitel got out, he was on the wrong side of the labor market. You do not pay a man one hundred or two hundred thousand dollars when he has a poor name politically and morally, a criminal record and an accelerating capacity for booze. When I first knew Eitel he worked on a script he planned someday to film and lived on very little in a shabby ranch house on the edge of the desert. One night, on his patio, he showed for me, on a borrowed projector, a print in sixteen milli-meter of one of his early films.

> EITEL
> *(While the film plays)*

Sergius, I didn't know a thing when I made this picture and yet somehow I knew more.

> SERGIUS

You'll do a movie like this again, champ.

> EITEL

I don't know. I can't get out of myself long enough to find where it's hiding in me. I feel as if I've been ampu-tated.

> *(He laughs)*

I had a girl the other night for the first time in three months and gave her five hundred dollars in celebration. Insanity! Kid, if I ever bring off this new movie of mine, remind me, will you, of this conversation. You see, I've been trying to remember if I was as depressed in the old days when the work would come out well.

Eitel saw very few people. One was a producer. Carlyle "Collie" Munshin.

"April is the cruellest month." I just thought of a great movie to waste. *The Wasteland* by T.S. What's-his-name?

Collie was the son-in-law of Herman Teppis . . . who was the head of Supreme Pictures.

You take the desert. It's a wonderful place to make a human being feel alive. I hear music in it all the time. A musical. It's full of cowboys and these fellows that live alone, what do you call them, hermits. Cowboys and hermits and pioneers, that's the sort of place it is; fellows looking for gold. I like history.

Yes, you must be ready with questions. Was Eitel sent here, you may ask, because he talked that way once long ago to a Senator? Is Collie Munshin here because he wants to wreck T.S. What's-his-name? Is it possible Herman Teppis is here, too? Is everybody in Hell? Were they always here or did they move here? My friends, waste no time trying to discover the rules, properties, proportions and schedules of Hell. If it took the Mysterious Power most of Eternity to invent this spectrum of punishment, do not expect to figure it out in one night. No! Stop working for the team. Relax. Sit back and enjoy yourselves.

57

There will be no devils—at least I don't think so—there will only be bad manners and bad morals. And self-confession. Watch as we come up to the footlights and say our piece and say our piece all alone.

(The tote board dances, which is to say: a symphony of numbers begins. 99, 88, and 44 predominate. (There are 44 changes in each act and 11 in the prologue.) Indeed all sorts of numbers might whip through, a ballet of numbers for the numerologically-oriented of the audience. Numbers—we whisper it— are the blood of technology—so the tote board is a reminder of the world's blood, for the world is a technology now. We end on 44. Change 44 is about to begin.)

What is that number? It means that I have just begun the bottle, but the prologue is gone.

(The cast leaves—it is as if they have been dispelled by a wave of the hand)

We are into the action just about. We are back at the crime, close again to the heart of that mirror— that icy silver from Hell—which reveals that love may be murder, and murder an act of love.
But do not feel intimidated. Never panic. Some of you may be offended by what you hear—a few of our ideas are dreadful—you may want to leave before this evening of torture and oppression is concluded.

Go. Make a disturbance on your exit. But don't step on your neighbor's feet or you may discover Hell is creeping up on you. Nothing gets you in Hell so fast as being a sneak.

(He starts to leave. Turns back)

One last word. Remember that I am known here as a young pilot back from the war, full of poker money and looking for a good time. Therefore, respect my privacy. Do not wave to me.

(Sergius winks, and steps into the action. He and Eitel are together. Munshin has just entered. We are— you may have divined it—begun.)

CHANGE FORTY-FOUR

MUNSHIN

I've decided to give the brush to my girl.

EITEL

What's the matter? Has Herman Teppis laid down the law?

MUNSHIN

Charley! This is a personal tragedy for me. I'm very worried about the girl's future.

EITEL

From what I've heard about her, she'll get along.

MUNSHIN

What did you hear?

EITEL

I'd rather not say.

59

MUNSHIN

Come on, Charley, give it to me. What did you hear?

EITEL

That when you're not around, your little kitten will go for a romp. By all reports she's a genius in the dark.

MUNSHIN

Scandal. This is a beautiful human being.

>*(Eitel laughs mockingly—he laughs mockingly indeed. Caution, outrage, and a profound respect for Munshin's chicanery are in the laughter. He knows Munshin is up to a plot, but what is the plot? And where?)*

I know. When I first set the girl up I thought, "Just another nightclub dancer." Well, she may not match up to some of the people I know.

>*(In an aside to Sergius)*

She lacks two things: class and distinction . . . but that doesn't keep her from being very human.

>*(Back to Eitel—in the categorical tones of a lawyer addressing every element in a jury)*

She's a girl who's composed of hurts and emotion and dirt and the irredesiessence of love. I had my analyst send her to a colleague friend of his but she didn't make much progress. Not enough ego to work on.

EITEL

Her analyst sent reports to you?

MUNSHIN

>*(Bypassing this hedgehog)*

She's a girl who's all hurts. The night I met her she was doing a fill-in number at a benefit I ran. I saw her in the wings. A real Carmen type. Only a Carmen shuddering with fright. "There's a human being in torment," I said to myself, "a girl who's as wild and sensitive as me."

60

EITEL
(To Sergius)
In the movie industry, this is known as love at first sight.

MUNSHIN
Eitel, you're remote. I can't reach you. Are you so ungrateful that I have to remind you how many times I pleaded with H.T. to let you make the kind of picture you wanted to make?

EITEL
(An old hatred breaking through)
And then you would cut it to ribbons.

MUNSHIN
We've had our disagreements, but, Charley, you're my friend. I need your opinion. What do you think of Elena the way I've described her?

EITEL
I think she's better than you deserve.

MUNSHIN
Glad you say that. It means I've been able to convey her quality. You see, about an hour ago I told Elena we were through.

EITEL
An hour ago? When is your wife due?

MUNSHIN
Tomorrow . . . all right, I'm no good. I'm scared. There's no telling what this girl will do. Charley, could you pay her a visit?

EITEL
No.

MUNSHIN
That girl should not be left alone. She'll feel she wasn't good enough for me.

EITEL
It's the truth, isn't it? That's how you feel.

MUNSHIN

Can't you sympathize?

EITEL

With you?

MUNSHIN

Could you pay her a visit? I told her I was coming to
see you.

EITEL

I don't even know her.

MUNSHIN

I'll introduce you as one of my dearest friends.

EITEL

It would be an unforgiveable slander.

MUNSHIN

Listen, if anything happens to this girl, it will be your
fault. Offer a solution at least.

EITEL

Turn her over to Marion Faye.

MUNSHIN

Marion Faye! You're a stone. A human being is in pain
and you suggest Marion Faye.

SERGIUS

I'll see her.

EITEL

Keep out of this.

MUNSHIN

You're a beautiful kid, but this is not the job for you.
Or maybe it is. Charley, tell me, are you getting too old to
handle a real woman . . . are you?

> *(The phone rings. Eitel picks up the
> phone. We hear the sound of a
> woman who is crying and laughing.
> Her hysteria quivers through the
> room. Rage in her voice and pain.*

*One cry, loud in its extremity, "You
Bastaaaaaard." For that moment,
Eitel does not yet know for whom
the voice is intended. It may be the
voice of a woman out of his own
past—the horror of sexual exploita-
tion stirs like the ghost of a charred
corpse; he is face to face with a
moment which is come to him
either from the depth of his own
past or speaks of the future. Then
in the next instant as Munshin takes
the phone, Eitel realizes the voice
had to belong to Elena. But, he is
shaken.)*

Elena, stay in your hotel room. I'll be right over.

EITEL

I'll come along if you wish.

MUNSHIN

It's okay. I'll call you tomorrow.

(He exits)

SERGIUS

How can any operator as smart as Munshin get into such
a mess?

EITEL

A little compassion, Sergius, do you think we choose our
mates?

(Lights fade)

CHANGE FORTY-THREE

TEPPIS

In my day a man got married and he could be fortunate
in his selection or he could have bad luck, but he was

63

married. I was a husband for thirty-two years, may my wife rest in peace, I have her picture on my desk. Can you say that? What do you have on your desk? Pin-up pictures. I don't know people who feel respect for society any more.

(Blackout)

CHANGE FORTY-TWO

(Light on Eitel smoking a cigarette on the patio. Elena, uncomfortable in the strong sunlight, comes out from the bedroom. She moves as if she feels unfresh.)

EITEL

Let's have coffee.

(When she nods sullenly, he goes on in a manner which is just a touch too animated, as if he is concealing his fever to put her in a good mood. It is, of course, important to him that she get into a good mood, or otherwise he will never comprehend their extravaganza of the night before.)

After we get a little food in us and feel human, we'll go for a drive. It'll pick you up.

ELENA

Don't worry about me, I'll get out.

(A note on the tender sentiments of the heroine. She has been ready twenty-four hours ago to—we will find out later what she was ready to do—but the sin she was contemplat-

64

ing could not have been more mortal. Then, last night, an act of love about which we are going to discover all sorts of intimations in the quickest time. Trust the combination to have left her in a state of true dread. She is in dread all through the first half of this scene. She does not play dread—she contains it. It is as if any gust of wind across the desert might carry any message of doom. So she is sullen, reserved, uncomfortable—she might fear that if Eitel rebuffs her, the pit will open again.)

EITEL

I didn't mean get out.

ELENA

Nothing ever works in the morning.

(Pause)

EITEL

Let's have coffee.

(Hands her a cup)

ELENA

I don't like to talk.

EITEL

Be a love. Tell me. Where did you get your green eyes?

ELENA

My mother is Polish. I'm half Polish and half Italian. Oil and water.

(Pause)

EITEL

Do you know, last night I thought we were meeting for the first time but this morning I have the feeling I've seen you before.

ELENA

You did. Once. But you weren't even really looking at me.

EITEL

I don't believe that's possible.

ELENA

Well, it's true. I was an extra once in a movie you made. I thought you'd see me and decide I was material for a star. But you said to me, "Honey, don't move too close to the camera, I don't want your distraction in this scene."

EITEL

I thought you were a flamenco dancer.

ELENA

I wanted to be. Once in a while my agent would get me a job for a couple of nights.

EITEL

Were you a good dancer? Of course you were.

ELENA

I could have made it if it hadn't been for Collie. He wanted me under lock and key in case he had a free hour.

EITEL

You stopped dancing?

ELENA

I danced in bed . . . I'm lazy. I'm lazy and Collie is stingy. We were a good pair.

> *(Her gift for irony may be unexpected, but it is not inconsiderable)*

EITEL

You must have brought out the best in each other.

ELENA
> *(The depression of her situation is suddenly and fully open upon her. From the pit of her hangover, she speaks.)*

The best.

(This, friends, is said with a lot of voice. The horror, the greed, the carnality, the piggishness, the ambition, the appetite, the deception and the hatred of her affair with Munshin might sound in her voice. No less a task is there for the actress.)

. . . Jesus, it was exceptionally low of Collie to dump me in this town.

EITEL

What is there to keep you from going back to the city?

ELENA

I don't know anybody in the city.

EITEL

You don't know anybody in the city?

ELENA

I don't make friends. Women don't flock to me, dig? and I make men nervous. I didn't get into the kind of thing with most ladies and gentlemen where I would want to see them again.

EITEL

No family?

ELENA

Before I pick up the phone to call my bitch of a mother, I would go to hell.

EITEL

You're a proud little girl in your way.

ELENA
(Furious at the condescension)
And you're a dumb fuck.

EITEL

I was wondering how you might describe me.

ELENA
(For the first time, her voice reveals

67

vulnerability. A tenderness of the fiercest proportions is only half-buried in her.)

I wouldn't talk about you.

(Eitel looks away, but the question comes)

Why, would you talk about me?

EITEL

Only if I were being psychoanalyzed.

(He smiles, she begins to giggle. In a moment they are both laughing. The laughter is a negotiation. Do they each keep trading? As a lock is opened in one, does the other turn a key?)

ELENA

And lose your lip?

(Now the laughter dies out. An inner debate. Can this new magnifico be trusted? Elena plunges. Eitel is promoted on the spot to Intimate.)

Listen, I was always asking my analyst about Collie. I wanted to learn how to make Collie think I loved him.

EITEL

Did you succeed?

ELENA

No.

EITEL

You fired the analyst.

ELENA

I stopped going. Two weeks ago. My analyst made a pass at me. Boy, were his hands clammy. I guess he was afraid of losing his license. I owed him eight hundred and fifty

68

bucks, which Collie finally coughed up for me to pay. But I didn't pay him after he made that pass. My shrink screwed me up. So I kept the loot. I deserved it. When I think of some of the crazy things I used to go out and get into, just so I could be more interesting to my doctor. You know, so he'd write me up as a case or something.

EITEL
(*Trying not to wince at her character*)

How did Collie take all this?

ELENA

He'd have forgiven me if I'd let him make home movies.

EITEL

You think you have a better character than Collie?

ELENA

I wouldn't say that. I've done some way-out things.

EITEL

Way-out?

ELENA

Pretty far.

EITEL

More of the way-out than last night?

ELENA
(*Moved to a depth of admission by his final readiness to stand or fall on the depth of the event on the night before*)

Oh, you're good. You know you're good . . .

(*Pouring him an imaginary and not altogether innocent glass of champagne*)

why, you're a champion.

EITEL

I'm a professional anyway.

(Smiles)

Beware of love.

ELENA

I don't love anybody.

EITEL

Nobody?

ELENA

Once in a while I think I'm fantastic.

EITEL

Good way to feel.

(Says the next speech lightly)

Do you think we ought to try it for a few days?

ELENA

It wouldn't work with you.

EITEL

Why not find out?

ELENA

Find out what?

(Hint of heartbreak)

That the second night is never as good as the first. Look, you do what you want. I'll do what I want.

EITEL

Need money . . . ?

ELENA

Not now. My analyst kissed me!

(They laugh)

EITEL
(In the candor which follows a second good laugh)

70

Let me warn you that I'm really a very cold man.

ELENA
(Starts to go, pauses)
You're full of emotion.

*(They are caught in this moment by
the fading of the lights)*

CHANGE FORTY-ONE

(Light on Teppis)

TEPPIS
Listen, do you know how many of the most successful
marriages in this industry started with just publicity? I'll
tell you. The answer is ninety-nine percent of the most
successful marriages began just that way. It's like a dowry
in the old country.

(Blackout)

CHANGE FORTY

---

*(Lights again on Eitel's patio. Eitel
alone. Marion enters.)*

EITEL
Why today? I haven't seen you in weeks.

MARION
You were making the rounds with Elena last night. I
wanted to see Collie's girl.

EITEL
Curious?

MARION
Collie is a collector. Anything he keeps for three years is
interesting to me.

71

EITEL

I won't ask you to leave her alone—I don't think you could move in on her.

MARION

Oh, I could. I could whistle and she would hear it from a mile away. Have a little respect for human experience.

EITEL

The experience of a pimp?

MARION

Charley, I know more than the President of the United States, and so does a nigger whore.

EITEL

Did you ever consider why you're doing this bit?

MARION

Tell me, beloved.

EITEL

Panic. All-out, unadulterated, homosexual panic.

MARION

Homosexual panic. You're the one to talk.

EITEL

I am. For me the worst part of prison was the sex. I chose to stay away from that, from all of that. I didn't see why I should start at this late date.

MARION

It left you middle-aged, baby.

EITEL

You. When you were in prison you ran amok.

MARION

I used to worry I was queer. Now I know I'm only half-queer.

EITEL

Half-queer, and without dignity.

72

MARION

You have your dignity and you feel . . . amputated.

> *(It is as if he summons the word
> from Eitel's previous conversation
> with Sergius)*

EITEL

I did. I did until last night.

MARION

Come on, Charley, for fifteen years you couldn't make
a picture without being king of the hay. And now you
flip over a chick who used to tickle Collie Munshin's little
itches.

EITEL

I'd prefer it if you didn't talk about her that way.

MARION

What talent Elena must have. Man, you are laying the
foundations of a monumental mistake.

EITEL

You have a mechanical mind. It comes from too much
screwing.

MARION

Maybe I wouldn't hear all the jazz you hear, lover, but I
can develop her talent. Do you have enough to develop her
talent?

EITEL

Maybe I've been given something I never had before.

MARION

You're spoiled. Once you could make love to a woman
and the sugar of your reputation would make her warm
and open before you moved a finger. Now you're an ex-con
who can't get a job and doesn't have any real dough left
and you want to keep a girl who was born to travel in a
big league. Hard times ahead, Charley, and maybe I'll just
demonstrate it to you.

73

(Exits—Eitel is left alone)

(Death music comes in faintly. It will be heard again near the very end of the play, "a wisp of fog, all too soon a vapor." Eitel speaks almost in an aside.)

EITEL

I knew the moment I met her I would make love to her. It was that simple, and I thought it was going to be that unimportant. A hot babe. Might I prove worthy. Instead, something flew in like a madman on wings. An angel. For the first time in my life I felt as if there were some sweet substance to be found in love, not power, but the sweetest thing I'd ever known—heaven. I was desperate in the morning that I might lose her. It was as if God had touched me with a finger, and I didn't want to lose that sensation ever again.

(Fade)

CHANGE THIRTY-NINE

TEPPIS

A big red heart. The American public has a big red heart. And you got to meet it, you got to go halfway up to it.

(Blackout)

CHANGE THIRTY-EIGHT

(Spotlight on Elena as she picks up the receiver in her hotel room—she is sitting on Marion's lap)

ELENA

Oh, darling, is something the matter?

74

EITEL

Nothing. It's just that I want to hear your voice.

ELENA

But Charley, at this hour?

EITEL

Listen, you wouldn't want to come over here now, would you?

ELENA

Honey, I'm tired.

EITEL

Oh well, forget it.

ELENA

You're not angry?

EITEL

Of course not.

ELENA

I'm so sleepy.

EITEL

I shouldn't have called. You go back to bed.

ELENA

I missed you tonight, but it'll be nice tomorrow.

EITEL

Tomorrow. I missed you, too.

> *(Lights fade first on Eitel as he hangs up. Marion takes the phone from Elena, hangs up. She follows him as the light fades.)*

CHANGE THIRTY-SEVEN

(Lights on Eitel's patio. Eitel is pac-
ing about. He stops when Elena en-
ters.)

EITEL

Were you alone last night?

ELENA

I want to talk to you about that. Your friend asked me for
a date.

EITEL

Which friend?

ELENA

Marion Faye.

EITEL

You had a casual date.

ELENA

A little more than that.

EITEL

You mean a lot more than that.

ELENA

Yes, sort of.

EITEL

I guess I haven't been your particular number

ELENA

How you talk.

EITEL

Still, you had something left in reserve?

ELENA

You're enjoying this.

76

EITEL

Elena! Why did you do it?

ELENA

I was curious.

EITEL

I could kill you.

(The meaning is passionate, but not the tone of voice. Eitel is still in command of himself. It is almost a dry suggestion—Yes, I could kill you. By ants perhaps or bamboo slivers beneath the skin.)

ELENA

But I want to tell you . . .

EITEL

Yes, what?

ELENA

I felt like a statue with him.

EITEL

Only you didn't act like a statue with him.

ELENA

Well . . . I thought of you all the time.

EITEL

(His contained rage is violent, his control is superb)

A whore can always create a diversion.

ELENA

You don't care about me. You don't really care. Just your pride is hurt.

EITEL

(The first crack shows)

How in hell could you do it?

ELENA

You think I'm stupid.

77

EITEL

You are stupid.

ELENA

When a woman's unfaithful, she's more attractive to a man.

EITEL

Stop reciting your lessons.

ELENA

It's not lessons. I know . . .

EITEL

You don't know anything. Don't you understand? I believe I love you. I, Jesus by God, love you. I love your body.

ELENA

You love my body, but you don't love me.

EITEL
(In the soup now)

I love you.

ELENA

I worship you. It's better with you than it's been with anyone.

(Fade)

CHANGE THIRTY-SIX

(Lights on Teppis)

TEPPIS

One of the most heart-warming customs of the people I was born in, was the concern the parents of the family took in all the doings of their children, the engagements, the weddings, the births of young people. I was talking to my friend, the Pasha Bey Omi Kin Bek on this very subject and you know what he said to me, he said, "H.T., we don't arrange marriages the way the American public ·tends to think, we Sultans just encourage them and then it's up to the kids." I could tell you stories make you cry.

(Lights fade)

CHANGE THIRTY-FIVE

(Lights on Eitel's patio. Elena napping, alone. Marion enters, wakes her with a proprietory whack on her rump.)

ELENA

Charley isn't here.

MARION

It's you I want to talk to.

ELENA

Marion, we don't have a hell of a lot to say.

MARION

You're a liar. It was all the way for me last time, and so it was for you.

ELENA

I never felt so low in my life as I felt after you. You're the gutter. Now, get out. Charley is the one I want to make it with.

MARION

You make your nest with a middle-aged man.

ELENA

You think I stay with him because he's good to me?

MARION

He's your nurse.

ELENA

He's my lover . . . he's my lover. I never could use that

79

word before. Not for other men, not for you. But he's my lover. When he touches me . . .

MARION

You are ready to conceive at the next touch.

ELENA

Crazy. You know about love.

MARION

I know about sex, cunt-head. I feel that for a hundred men and women.

ELENA

And a dog or two.

MARION

And a dog or two. And you got the dog in you. Let's give Eitel that. He turned you on. He turned you on and he'll leave you. You have no future with Eitel.

ELENA

He loves me.

MARION

He's a snob. Whatever he has, whatever he owns, sooner or later he comes to detest it because it's his and so it can't be good. Nothing less than a princess could bring him joy.

(Quick fade)

CHANGE THIRTY-FOUR

TEPPIS

You know what an artist is? He's a crook. They even got a Frenchman now, you know what, he picks people's pockets at society parties. They say he's the greatest writer in France. No wonder they need a dictator, those crazy French. I could never get along with the French.

(Quick fade)

CHANGE THIRTY-THREE

(A note from the playwright to the reader: Love occurs as a word nine times in the scene which follows. We are obviously in the presence of a comic mood or a bad one, for our two pioneers are embarked on a reconnaissance up the headwaters of the ancient Amazonic mystery— our old buddy—Love. Change Thirty-three for your pleasure.)

ELENA

You can't love me. I don't come from nothing at all.

EITEL
(Now, witness: Eitel is trying to work. His script is open. He has been rewriting a passage whose quality has always eluded him. Closes script—brusque.)

You never tell me anything about where you come from.

ELENA
(Guarded)

What's to tell? My father was a small-time hood. There's nothing worse. And my mother . . .

(She pauses. Emotion has stolen up on her.)

EITEL

Tell me.

ELENA

A greedy little flirt. She ended up nothing but a fat ass.

81

(To justify her last remark, Elena goes on)

She was always complaining that life left her in a candy store.

EITEL

That's a cruel life.

(He cannot resist returning to his script)

ELENA

Cruel! It was a farce. She would take me when I was a kid and say, "If you don't do nothing else, get off this God-damn street." Then five minutes later, she'd slap me so hard I'd almost fall down.

(Turns and sees him immersed in work)

Charley, you want out, don't you?

EITEL

What gives you these ideas?

ELENA

I was just thinking you were sick of me.

(Pause)

EITEL

(He closes the script again)

Elena, what's really the matter?

ELENA

A man followed me today . . . He had the evil eye.

EITEL

I'm sure he wanted to cut off your head and stuff you in a gunny sack.

ELENA

That's what you'd like to do to me. Good Time Charley. You only like me when I'm in a good mood.

EITEL

Good Time Charley. When I say nice things then you love me.

ELENA

You're so superior. But you don't know what goes on in my head. I want to become a nun.

EITEL

Are you crazy? You'd make a honey of a nun.

ELENA

A nun is never alone. Nuns always have company.

EITEL

Do I ruin everything I touch?

> (*He is all but enjoying himself. It is like some scene in the sort of soap opera he would tune out—except that the actors have gone surrealistic. They are saying, "Up your buns" to the sponsor.*)

Why are you so unhappy if I love you?

ELENA

I don't think you get to be in love unless you deserve it. Otherwise you get the evil eye.

EITEL

Do I deserve love?

ELENA

You bet you do.

EITEL

But you don't deserve it?

ELENA

Will you still love me if I cut my hair? No, you won't.

EITEL

If my love depends on a haircut, you might as well find out now.

ELENA

Yes, I ought to find out.

EITEL

You're a child.

ELENA

Kiss me, Charley.

(They embrace)

I'm going to leave you someday, Charley, I mean it.

EITEL

I don't know why.

ELENA

Charley, did you know I read all that crazy testimony of yours years ago in the newspapers?

EITEL

No, you never told me.

ELENA

Well, I read it. And so did a lot of kids I know. Actors, showgirls, just friends. Oh, Charley, it cracked us up. You were not afraid and everyone we knew was so crummy and scared. I felt horrible when you went to jail. I remember I even said to Collie, "I'd like to meet Charles Francis Eitel, he's a real man and there aren't many left."

EITEL

(Moved by the generosity of her admission, by its pompous naïveté, by the intriguing fact that she had been talking once to Collie about him, and that offered explanations as well)

I don't offer you anything now, do I?

ELENA

I don't think about it, why do you?

EITEL

Because you're a woman. You have to think about it.

84

If I worried because you didn't offer . . . anything, it would mean I didn't really love you.

(They embrace)

Oh Charley, you're a king. When you make love to me, everything is all right again.

(A shadow of the future intervenes again)

But I'm so afraid.

(Fade)

CHANGE THIRTY-TWO

TEPPIS

What am I showing you? Two hands. Two hands make a body. You see, I feel as if I come from two faiths, the one I was born with and the one I changed to and elected. I think I've inherited the wealth of tradition from two great faiths. Am I confusing you?

(Lights fade)

CHANGE THIRTY-ONE

(A scream is heard)

SERGIUS

Lulu was a heavy reader. She always had her nose in print. She never missed an item in the gossip columns.

LULU

(A scream of mingled delight and pain)

85

Listen to this! Just listen to this! "What do we hear about red-tainted Charley Eitel doing a boudoir Pygmalion with the protégée of a certain extra-but-big producer?" Oh, that Eitel! He never had any taste. Any tramp who tells him he's terrific can always sell him a ticket to her favorite charity!

SERGIUS

I like Elena.

LULU

You would. I bet she has dirty underwear. Watch! She's going to be fat as a bull.

SERGIUS

> Then she discovered an item about her and me.

> *(Lulu screams again)*

> It was an amazing item. Any newspaper publisher would have been proud to print it because the story did not contain a single line of truth, and that's a purity which is not easy to achieve.

LULU

Oh, Sergius, love, listen to this. "Atom Bomb Lulu Meyers and the potential next Mr. Meyers, ex-Marine Corps Captain, Silligus McShonessy . . ."

SERGIUS

Ex-Marine Corps Captain? Silligus McShonessy?

LULU

Ssssh. "Ex-Marine Corps Captain Silligus McShonessy, scion of an Eastern-or-is-it-Midwestern fortune . . ."

SERGIUS

Fortune!

LULU

". . . are setting off those geiger counters in Desert D'Or."

86

SERGIUS

Can't they get my name right?

LULU

You know, that's not bad. Atom Bomb Lulu Meyers. Do you think people really think of me that way?

SERGIUS

Of course they don't. You know your press agent wrote it.

LULU

I don't care, it's still interesting. Oh, sugar, they make us sound so good in the newspapers. Isn't it a wonderful life?

(Court dance strikes up. Sergius takes Lulu by the hand)

CHANGE THIRTY

SERGIUS

Lulu and I, we made the rounds.

TEPPIS

(Interrupting)

Wait! What's your name?

SERGIUS

Silligus McShonessy . . . I mean, Sergius O'Shaugnessy.

TEPPIS

What kind of a name is that for a clean-cut boy like you? John Yard! That's what you should call yourself. What do you do, I hope you're not a bum!

(Blackout on Teppis)

SERGIUS

We made the rounds. We had our little fights. We even made love when I could trick her into it.

CHANGE TWENTY-NINE

LULU

Do I look good without makeup?

SERGIUS

You look very good.

LULU

My mouth's a little too thin.

SERGIUS
(Riding hard on the memory)

It wasn't last night.

LULU

A corpse would satisfy you.

(Quick fade)

CHANGE TWENTY-EIGHT

*(Lights on Teppis. He is not look-
ing directly at Lulu, yet everything
in this speech is for her benefit. It
is as if she hears him in her mind.)*

TEPPIS

Let me show you psychology. Ten years ago, a woman she
was faithful to her husband, she wanted excitement, she
wanted to dream she was having a big affair with a star
—today, you know what, that same woman she has boy-
friends all over the place with the man who fixes the
television set, people like that. You think she wants to see
somebody just like herself on the screen somebody just as
nuts as she is? She don't. She's ashamed of herself. She

wants to see a woman she can respect, a married woman. That's true psychology.

(Fade)

CHANGE TWENTY-SEVEN

LULU

You'll end up hating me. You will. Nobody likes me who really knows me. Even I don't like myself.

SERGIUS

You love yourself.

LULU

It's not the same thing.

(Quick dim out and in)

SERGIUS

One day she declared she was going to take acting lessons.

CHANGE TWENTY-SIX

LULU

I'm going to begin from the very beginning. I'm going to learn how to walk and to breathe. I've never been properly trained, Sergius, did you know that?

SERGIUS

You'll never take lessons.

LULU

Of course I will. I'm going to be the greatest actress who ever lived. That's what nobody understands.

(Quick dim out and in)

CHANGE TWENTY-FIVE

SERGIUS

All the while we were waiting, the date when she would have to begin work on her new picture came closer. Once she told me that her co-star Teddy Pope

(Spotlight on Teddy)

and a featured actor named Tony Tanner

(Spotlight on Tony)

would be down at the resort for publicity photos with her.

CHANGE TWENTY-FOUR

(Spot on Teppis looking at Teddy)

TEPPIS

A rumor about a fellow like you, it spreads like hot cakes. We got letters from your fan clubs all over the place. Kokoshkosh, towns like that. Small-town America. Two-Bits, Kansas. You see what I mean? What do you want? You know what those letters say, they say that the members of the Teddy Pope fan club are brokenhearted 'cause they heard the most terrible stories about Teddy.

(Blackout Teppis)

SERGIUS

The new picture would be a triangle. Teddy Pope was to get her in the end, but through the middle of

the film she was to think she was in
love with Tony Tanner.

CHANGE TWENTY-THREE

LULU

Look at this photograph!

SERGIUS

What's wrong with it?

LULU

Tony Tanner looks better than me. They ought to shoot
the photographer. He's probably in Tony's employ.

SERGIUS
(Studying photograph)
You don't look so miserable with Tony's arm on you.

LULU

Why that's just publicity. I can't stand Tony.

(Blackout)

CHANGE TWENTY-TWO

---

*(Lights on Teppis. He is staring un-
abashedly across the stage at Lulu.)*

TEPPIS

Know what a star is? She's like a delicious perishable
fruit. You got to take her a long distance to market, and
when she's there, you got to sell her. If you don't she
rots. She's rotten. Lulu, I'm speaking to you like a
man to a woman. Believe me, Lulu, as God is looking
into this room you've made enemies, hundreds of enemies.
If you don't start to cooperate, they'll get into the process
of tearing your flesh and picking your bones. I don't want

91

to depress you, but, Lulu, your Bimmler has got to show improvement this coming year. Otherwise, there's only one way for you. The way is down. You'll go down and you'll go down.

(Blackout)

CHANGE TWENTY-ONE

LULU

I don't want to be silly about it. Naturally, I have to be seen with Teddy and Tony all the time. The studio wants lots of advance publicity on this picture.

SERGIUS

I guess I won't be seeing much of you.

LULU

That's ridiculous. You can be with us all the time. It's just that when they start to take pictures· it would be better if you sort of dropped out of sight.

(Quick dim out and in)

CHANGE TWENTY

SERGIUS

Now that Teddy and Tony had arrived, our life changed. We made a tour of the supper clubs and the nightclubs, Teddy going as escort to Lulu while Tony Tanner and I followed behind. Lulu was enchanted to be divided among three men.

92

CHANGE NINETEEN

SERGIUS

I wonder which Lulu you like the most.

LULU

The one with you, of course. What a bore Tony is.

(Lights stay)

CHANGE EIGHTEEN

(Teddy and Tony join them at a nightclub table, Tony inserting himself almost immediately between Sergius and Lulu. Teddy and Lulu exchange smiles of the brightest toothpaste and Teddy then takes up his station near Sergius, who ignores him, and proceeds instead to tap Tony Tanner briskly on the shoulder.)

SERGIUS

I understand you know Marion Faye.

TONY

That bastard. A couple of bimbos I used to have around did a little work for him. So now the word's out that I pimped. Can you beat that? That's the kind of thing that happens just when you're starting to make it big in the industry.

SERGIUS

You want to make it big, don't you?

TONY

What else? Don't you? I never will, though. I'll never make it, laddie.

SERGIUS

You never know. You might just make it.

TONY

I got a scandal. There was this screwball I used to live with and she was nuts about me. Only she was hopeless. I carried her as long as I could and then I told her to flake off. You know what? She killed herself. Believe it or not, I wanted the best for that little chicken. What a break. They say I drove her to it.

LULU

You're a bland boy.

TONY

Bland? Honey, I'm mellow. I enjoy a Mello-roll every day.

LULU

I bet you faint on the doorstep.

TONY

Your sweet little doorstep? Let me in and I'll Simonize your floor.

TEDDY
(Sergius starts to rise. Teddy intercepts him)

It's a pity you're afraid of me. Still a shy aviator, I see. I hate to camp but for some reason you bring it out in me.

SERGIUS
After a couple of days of this, I discovered that the wise money in Desert D'Or was laying five to two that Tony was in Lulu's bed and Teddy was in mine.

(Lights stay)

94

CHANGE SEVENTEEN

TEDDY

Is it true that most of you fliers live for drinking and sex?

SERGIUS

We live for anything that's good for our reflexes.

(A loud voice in Tony's ear)

I like reflexes more than I like people.

TONY

All right, kids, break it up. Lulu can't even hear me whisper in her ear.

(Well, that's the gauntlet, gang)

CHANGE SIXTEEN

SERGIUS

Let's go outside and have a little talk.

TONY

Talk before an audience. It stimulates me.

> *(Tony launches abruptly into a mock karate attack on Sergius with jabs, stabs, kicks, and karate cries, halting one inch from the neck and nuts. It is not however successful in causing psychic paralysis. Not altogether.)*

SERGIUS

You're very stimulating. With a crowd around you. You going outside or are you going to sit here and let me give the little talk?

95

LULU

Stop it, Sergius. This is brutal. You were in the Golden Gloves.

TONY

Well, you didn't mention that little detail, did you?

(Picking up wind now that he's home free)

Why not go outside? Only when you take care of me, you better take good care, because if you don't kill me, I've got a couple of friends who'll be looking for you.

(They are now each afraid of the other)

SERGIUS

Oh, let's go.

LULU

Stop!

(To Teddy and Tony)

Go away, both of you, just go away.

(Tony and Teddy leave. Tony with a snort, Teddy blowing one champion of a kiss. Lights narrow down to Lulu and Sergius.)

CHANGE FIFTEEN

LULU

It's awful, it's awful.

SERGIUS

What's awful?

LULU

I can't stand Tony. I hate his vulgarity, don't you, sugar? He makes me vulgar, too. That's what's so disgusting.

CHANGE FOURTEEN

(The lights dim and come up. Lulu is sitting alone with Sergius. She seems a hint depressed.)

LULU

Will you still love me if I let my hair go dark?

SERGIUS

You mean you weren't born a blonde?

LULU

Oh, I was born blonde, but my parents didn't always get along, so my hair turned dark.

SERGIUS

You're still a blonde. A blonde is a dame who chooses to be blonde because she's an optimist.

LULU

You mean that?

SERGIUS

Of course.

LULU

I know why I love you. You're a philosopher.

SERGIUS

A blonde is a dame who chooses to be blonde so much that she's a blonde even if the hair falls off from peroxide and she has to wear a blonde wig.

(Certain errors are cataclysmic. This has been one of them.)

LULU

Sergius, you have the right to know. I've been humiliated. I slept with Tony Tanner.

SERGIUS

But where? When?

LULU

In a telephone booth.

(Blackout)

SERGIUS

Now I had nine little men in me. I was miserable. It was possible I had really lost Lulu. She was never in when I called. And that was a blow to my sweet ego. Because one hundred million American men were no longer hating my guts.

CHANGE THIRTEEN

(Another word from the playwright: the transition in this scene is abrupt. It is, in fact, vertiginous. All disasters to come are buried in this dialogue, and the mood of the staging does well to give a hint that the gears of the drama are shifting down, that the extraordinary freedom of swinging from one bout of love to another has now brought us to a time of recapitulation and consequence. For the scene will end in a curse.)

SERGIUS

Sometimes my imagination invades my memory and I think I am each of these people speaking to me, speaking to you.

98

EITEL

(It is very late at night. Eitel comes out on his patio and stretches his arms luxuriously. There is an unexpected sound of amusement from Marion. Eitel has not known he was there.)

The next time you arrive in the hour before dawn, un-invited and conceivably unwanted, try ringing the bell.

MARION

You're Victorian, Charley. Nobody rings the bell.

EITEL

You wouldn't know how to get into a house if there was no lock to pick.

MARION

Charley, I couldn't sleep tonight, and all the while I knew you couldn't sleep either. Let me be your friend once more.

EITEL

I don't know that anything can be comfortable between us now.

MARION

Forgive me. Forgive this criminal for one crime against his dearest friend.

EITEL

I could forgive the devil tonight.

MARION

There's a question in my mind. It won't let me rest. Charley, you never gave one real lick for politics and yet you're the one who stood up to them.

EITEL

That's what keeps you awake?

MARION

Oh, I put down politics. But that was crazy testimony, Grand Duke. I hadn't liked you in years, suddenly I did.

99

EITEL

You mean it?

MARION

It gave me balls.

EITEL

There's your answer.

MARION

You were losing yours?

EITEL

I was going with two movie stars at the time. They were hot in the box office and I was hot for them. The thought of those royal ladies with their legs in the air had been my fuel for months. But when the moment came—Charles Francis Eitel was a dud. First one then the other. *Nada*. That happens to some men when they're young; it happened late to me. I began to think that impotence was no psychological aberration.

MARION

Don't go abstract, Charley.

EITEL

I'll give it to you straight. A young man can make love to a woman even if he's afraid of her husband—he's got the legs to run away, he still has the sweet gambling money of sex. But a man who's older knows that he must stand and face the other man if it comes to that. So you don't queer the corners. You make love to that which you are willing to fight for, or what will you settle for.

MARION

You're getting hip, Charley.

EITEL

Thank you. What came to me was that I had used up my gambling money and I hadn't won what was right for me. I had a talent and wasn't using it. You know what talent is? It's love. If you get love for nothing, you must give it back. But I never did, not really. I half-gave it back with movies which told too little.

100

MARION

You're nineteenth century, Charley, that's your charm.

EITEL

I prefer the eighteenth century before all style began to die.

MARION

You don't understand the eighteenth century. The eighteenth century was queer, friend. I mean, a friend made it with a friend, and then they both took the lady of either. It gave everybody a little life.

EITEL

You see all ladies as the devil.

MARION

I never argue about particulars. Who cares what is which? I tell you two celestial beings equally divine are caught in some marriage of mutual hate which spawned us poor crawling cells and all we do is part of their dance. Dig sex, Charley, that's all there is. Follow it to the end, professor. Turn queer, bang dogs, sniff toes, it don't matter, beloved. If you got the guts to follow it you pass through the eye of death. There's murder waiting for anybody who tries to ball his sex into charge. Cheer up, Charley, I'm really a man, I want what every man wants. No matter what I do, no matter how far out I go, or how low down I sink in the etiquette of the bed, I live for one thing, to bring ecstasy to a goddess and rule the world.

EITEL

You have captured the essence of Napoleon—Dear God, why do you talk so much?

MARION

I'm saying you're too yellow, Charley, to go to bed with me.

EITEL

I'd never let a man touch me. I think that's the death of . . . change. It's what all the people who run the machine want us to be. Queer. Queer as cockroaches. Once you

101

want it from behind, there's nothing to do but run. Thanks a lot, angel, but I don't want to swish.

MARION

When one man loves another it gives back heart to take it from behind. We have to take it from each other in order to dare the fury of a murderous cunt. I love you.

EITEL

No.

MARION

You want me, Charley.

EITEL

Never. I've got Elena.

MARION

I doubt it, grandfather.

EITEL

You don't seem to follow me very well. She is good for my body. She is the first woman who was ever good for me and God knows how many hundred I went through to discover that.

MARION

You've always seen yourself as an unattractive man.

EITEL

That's true, I did.

MARION

Your middle is thick. Do you see how slim I am.

EITEL

Don't strut.

MARION

I don't. I state the truth.

(Places one hand on his lower abdomen, one on his buttocks)

There is a life between my hands which you cannot understand. It is magical. It leads me. It charms me. It draws others to me. You don't possess that. That's why you feel unattractive.

EITEL

There is rhythm and there is warmth. You know more of one, I know more of the other.

MARION

Amateurs talk of warmth. Of decency. Of love. I talk of beauty. My mother was a beauty, *as you know*. I've known how to use sex since I was twelve. I bring good or I bring harm to anybody I cross.

EITEL

That kind of sex is a magnetism about as powerful, mysterious and meaningless as an electric current. But there is something else. You will not know what I talk about until it happens.

MARION

Love.

EITEL

Love.

MARION

Take love. Take all the love in the world. That's Bullshit Mountain.

EITEL

Orthodox Jews used to talk of the Shechinah. The Shechinah is the bride of God and she lives in exile—she is sundered from God. God is in search of his wife—who is missing. The Jews used to believe that when a man and wife make love, and were in love, that the bride of God was present. The Shechinah was there. So the act gave an echo of the heavens whether the man was fat or thin.

MARION

I never knew you were Jewish.

EITEL

Half-Jewish—both sides.

MARION

You once told me your mother was a French maid.

EITEL

The only time I feel close to the truth is when I tell a lie.

MARION

Daddy-O, listen to the truth. Elena is not right for you. You will kill yourself if you persist in the idea you're the best she's ever known in bed.

EITEL

Watch out. Your nerve is vicious but queer.

MARION

You really think I'm queer. Let me tell you. I never had a thing with a man till I went to prison. Till then it was just a matter of style, a clue to the science of sex. But in jail they got to me. Those cats were ugly—you think it didn't take guts to go to bed, it took balls, baby, balls. Some of those spades would have slit my throat if I made the wrong move at the right time. Kid you not, Daddy-O, I found my true guts in prison because I got to give it to an ape of a Mafia murder and he loved me like a whore. That turned the day, sahib, I've been flying ever since. Women never circled around me so much as they do now. Of course Elena digs me. Dig, you poor old dad, she reminds me of my Mafia ape who I turned into a little whore. Baby, I'll clue you: the night she spent with me gave her rhythms it'll take you years to digest.

EITEL

You murderous little faggot . . .

MARION

Charley, I don't want to find out who has the muscle . . .

EITEL

Get out before I throw you out.

Because when I let go, somebody is going to be dead.

(He exits)

CHANGE TWELVE

EITEL

I had an affair with Marion's mother—years ago. We almost married because of Marion. He was just a little boy really—spoiled, bright, sensitive, too pretty for his own good. But he was the first human being I wanted to make better than me. And then I broke with Dorothea. But it wasn't Dorothea I deserted—it was Marion.

ELENA

I'm glad he's gone. That son of a bitch would drink my blood.

(Blackout)

CHANGE ELEVEN

(The following dialogue is internal. It could be staged with Eitel's back to Marion or with Marion indeed invisible.)

EITEL

Why don't you believe I love her?

MARION

What do you want me to say? I'll say it.

EITEL

You see something in her yourself. She has such a need for dignity.

105

Dignity! Charley, you know like I know, she's just a girl who's been around.

That's not true. That's not all of it.

Do yourself a favor. Ask Elena if she ever did it for money.

What do you know?

> *(Says this so loudly that Elena starts—as if surprised that he is speaking aloud and to himself)*

I don't know, Charley. I just got an instinct for this.

> *(Lights fade on Marion. If the production is using a bell or a gong, it could well start to sound now at the end of each Change.)*

CHANGE TEN

EITEL
> *(Brusquely turning to her)*

Elena, did you ever take money from a man?

ELENA

Never. Well, never exactly. Except for once.

EITEL

Except for once? How was that?

ELENA

That was a funny time.

106

EITEL

Yes? How did it happen?

ELENA

Well, there was a man, and he wanted to, and I refused, and then the man offered money, twenty dollars he offered.

EITEL

So what did you do?

ELENA

I took it. It made the man seem exciting to me.

EITEL

You're a dirty little girl.

ELENA
(Low and smoky)

Well, you know I am.

EITEL

Yes.

ELENA

I enjoyed spending the twenty dollars.

EITEL

It didn't bother you?

ELENA

No.

EITEL

It bothered you.

ELENA

I got hysterical the next night, but I'm loused up anyway. Charley, let's not talk about it.

EITEL

Who was the man?

ELENA

Never mind.

107

EITEL

It was Collie.

ELENA

Somebody you never met.

EITEL

Twenty lousy bucks!

(Blackout—bell)

CHANGE NINE

(Lights on the patio. Lulu enters and circles Elena most leisurely, going around once, then twice, even if this takes thirty seconds.)

LULU

What do you do, Miss Esposé?

EITEL

Esposito.

ELENA

I've been . . . a dancer.

LULU

Get paid for it?

ELENA

No . . . I mean, of course not . . .

(In reaching for a cigarette, she knocks over the pack of cigarettes. General embarrassment, picking up, etc.)

LULU

They say you're through, Charley.

EITEL

They certainly do talk about me.

108

LULU

Not as much as you think. Time passes.

EITEL

I'll always be remembered as your second husband.

LULU

It's a fact. When I think of Charley Eitel, I think of Number Two.

(*Blackout—bell*)

CHANGE EIGHT

ELENA

You were comparing me to Lulu.

EITEL

No comparison.

ELENA

You were eating your heart out because once you were married to her and now you're down here with me. Nothing—living with nothing.

EITEL

She's not worth hating.

ELENA

Only you think she's better than you are.

EITEL

Elena, please stop shrieking like a fishwife.

ELENA

You call me a fishwife 'cause you can't screw your princess anymore.

EITEL

She's not a princess, she's just an actress.

ELENA

You got an itch. Go scratch it.

(Blackout—bell)

CHANGE SEVEN

MUNSHIN

Cupcake!

ELENA

How are you?

MUNSHIN

I don't exist for you any more, do I?

ELENA

You don't.

MUNSHIN

Lulu said to give you a message.

EITEL

Yes, what is that?

MUNSHIN

She said she feels sorry for you.

ELENA

I'm going shopping for eats.

EITEL

Come back here.

ELENA

Good-bye. You two can tell each other your dirty little secrets while I'm gone.

(She exits)

MUNSHIN

I should have warned you.

EITEL

The subject is not acceptable.

110

MUNSHIN

All right, let's get to the real point. I've got you by the short hairs. I read your script.

EITEL

How'd you get a copy?

MUNSHIN

You're trying to interest every European producer around to make it. What do you think? Listen, baby, I didn't have to run around the block with an egg in my shoe to get a copy. In Europe they're using your script to wipe their asses on.

EITEL

What I like about you, Collie, is that you never find a real point too delicate to make.

MUNSHIN

Listen, lover, it would cost five million to get quality into this property and nobody in Europe would trust you with half a million even if they had it. I'm here to discuss big American plans with you. But I can't start cold. You know me. The one snag in my productorial equipment is that I need a finger up my giggie to get started. Anal compulsive female identifications.

EITEL

Hush, little baby, don't you cry.

MUNSHIN

Charley, I would like a warm-up.

EITEL

Did you read it, or did one of your secretaries read it?

MUNSHIN

Charley, I read it. Trust me.

> *(Eitel nods profoundly at the thought of trusting Munshin)*

Alright, I'll tell *you* the story . . . and you'll get sick hearing me mangle it. You have a hero, a young ambitious man

111

who has a large television program. A prize-money show for the sick. He draws every cripple in our crazy country. They all come to tell their troubles on the air. And whichever package of horror and misery gives the most charge to the studio audience goes away with a bag of loot.

EITEL
(Looking up)
You're doing fairly well, Collie.

MUNSHIN
The hero converts suffering into mass entertainment. He becomes rich from the agony of the mob. Yet there comes a switch.

> *(Eitel makes a face, but Munshin goes on)*

A little door is opened in his heart, and through that door of goodness flows the waters of pain. His ears come attuned to the organ sounds of human misery. He starts to give real advice on the air—kill your mother, screw your brother—He's too honest—he destroys his program. In come the sponsors, enter the censors, make with the pressure. Your hero explodes, he attacks one of the Madison Avenue goons he's got in his hair, he almost kills him in his rage. Brouhaha!

EITEL
Alright, Collie, you've made your point. Let me tell it now.

MUNSHIN
Parenthetically, I can say this is a snitch from *Miss Lonelyhearts.*

EITEL
It was an influence.

MUNSHIN
Trust your unconscious, Charley. There's a religious revival underway in this country. So, thank God, your idea is practical.

112

EITEL

Shut up, let me take it from here . . .

> *(As he speaks, his voice takes on resonance)*

My hero goes to prison for assault and battery. Just a little time in the black hole but it changes him forever. For when he comes out, he seeks the bottom of the world—and he wanders through slums and soup kitchens and cheap dives, trying to be good to the people he sees, but he has spent too many years teaching them dishonesty.

> *(How can Eitel bother to tell his story thus formally? It is probably in protest against the pain of Munshin's telling. But it is more. He is still in love with his script. He must handle the story himself, even fondle it with his language.)*

Now dishonesty is the only passion they would defend to the death. So he comes to learn the taste of the cruellest defeat—that special private bitter taste which comes from losing when your motives are good. And so anger is born again and the murderous passion to win. He turns on these people of the bottom and is destroyed . . . But why am I telling this to you?

MUNSHIN

Extraordinary.

EITEL

You really like it?

MUNSHIN

It's an epic study about the hole in eternity our country is preparing for itself. It's a poem. This can make the greatest picture in the last ten years.

EITEL

Collie, why don't you say what you really think?

113

MUNSHIN
(Fingering his belly)

No audience would understand it.

EITEL

I think it would be amazing how much this would communicate to an audience.

MUNSHIN

You don't communicate with an audience, you manipulate an audience . . . Look, I love this story . . . and I know what it suffers from.

EITEL

What?

MUNSHIN

It's too hip. It's a whorehouse. Your hero is coining thousands of dollars a week and he decides to give it up. For what? To help people? To end suffering? He's a creep. They'll laugh your picture off the screen. You think an audience wants to pay money to be told this character is better than they are?

EITEL

What if guilt is real? What if all of us have intimations that we cannot cheat life forever, that if we live badly we go to some kind of hell where we must wait . . . agonies of time . . . before we are born again.

MUNSHIN

This is the idea behind all that crapalong, when your hero does his switch.

EITEL

Yes, all that crapalong.

MUNSHIN

Charley, it's not grounded. You can't turn a television host into a saint . . . Religion is institutional.

(Count one . . . two . . . three)

Eitel, the solution is simple . . . let your hero be a priest.

114

A priest!

Let's say he's only studying to be a priest—Brother Frederick. Personality-wise he has everything, charm, intelligence, poise—just one thing wrong . . . the guy's too cocky. I see a terrific scene where the principal or the head monk or whatever they call him at a priest school, a kind of wise old priest-type Irishman, calls in Freddie and tells the kid that it's no go, he doesn't think Frederick ought to become a priest, not yet. Scholastically, the kid's got everything. He's tops in Church History, in Bingo Management, he's A-plus in Confessional Psychology, but he doesn't have the heart of a priest. "Get out in the world, son, and learn humility," the old prick says. Do you see it now?

Colossal!

The kid takes the advice like a rejection. He feels unloved. So he quits the priest school, and goes into television, a bitter kid, he plays the angles. His career goes up like a sky rocket. Build him as a heel, and then give the switch. He discovers humility. I don't know what we can find, but I wouldn't even worry about it. Something with a Christ motif and the audience has to buy it. We can give Freddie a *Wanderjahr,* stumbling around bums with tears in his eyes, lots of business where he loves everybody. You get what I mean.

Colossal!

At the end Freddie doesn't have to die in the gutter, he can go back to the seminary and be accepted. An upbeat ending. Something with angels' voices in the background. Only not full of shit . . .

(Blackout—bell)

CHANGE SIX

(Lights on Teppis)

TEPPIS

It would take a talented director to make such a story. A fellow who knows the human heart. You take Eitel. Is he still hitting the booze? I wish he didn't have such a stain on his character. Bygones. Let it be bygones. I get along with everybody. I got no objection to making money with people I don't like. It's my motto.

(Blackout—bell)

CHANGE FIVE

MUNSHIN

Even if you won't sell your script to me, you still need money.

EITEL

I do. I want you to give me a short-term loan.

MUNSHIN

Against what?

EITEL

Black-market work. On any script but my own.

MUNSHIN

Beneath you, Charley. I pay thirty-five hundred dollars, no more, for a finished script when I supply the story.

EITEL

Lend me ten thousand. If I don't pay it back in three months, I owe you a script.

MUNSHIN

Charley, I'll give you thirty-five hundred.

EITEL

I don't want to exaggerate, but I feel as if you're pushing me to the wall.

MUNSHIN

When you go over the wall, I'll be there to catch you. I want you back, lover. Thirty-five hundred.

EITEL

Give me a choice.

MUNSHIN
(Counting out the cash)

Charley, I could cry every time I think of how you ruined your career.

EITEL
(Accepting money)

You cheap operator.

MUNSHIN

Call me any kind of crook you want, but just remember I'm the only crook in that cut-throat studio who cares two bits about you.

EITEL

I see a successful producer crying his heart out.

MUNSHIN
(In a low tone)

Damn you, Eitel, I didn't say I love you. I said I like you.

EITEL

That I might buy.

MUNSHIN

We could make a good team, you and me. We could just about run that studio.

EITEL

To suggest a partnership after the pennies you just tossed. You're more repulsive than you think.

117

MUNSHIN

You don't want charity, do you? I've been catching all the punches—Let me throw a few. You made a grandstand play a couple of years ago—and now you're whining over rough treatment. You're nothing but an infant prodigy. If you want big money, stop throwing curves to Congressional Committees and night-court magistrates.

EITEL

You want me to walk over to Herman Teppis, kiss his ass, apologize to the newspapers of America, and get taken back by the industry.

MUNSHIN

(Once again Munshin will bypass a hedgehog)

Listen, Dorothea is giving a party. You're invited.

EITEL

I know about that party. It's in honor of a dozen people I despise.

MUNSHIN

You give me a pain in the pecker. If you weren't so pure. It takes a speck of real dirt to cook up real art, don't you know that? Stop working both sides of the street. Eat a little dregs and be able to bargain with me, equal to equal, or face it, friend, you can settle down into a nice lower-middle-class life with Elena for your bride.

EITEL

Let's not start talking about Elena.

MUNSHIN

You feel two ways about her, don't you?

EITEL

Yes, brother, two ways.

(Blackout—bell)

118

CHANGE FOUR

(Lights on Teppis)

TEPPIS

Now, I'm a polite fellow. I wouldn't even be rude to my doorman. But you know something? They all cut my throat. You know something? My throat don't cut.

(Blackout—bell)

CHANGE THREE

EITEL

There're times when the knowledge of how Elena would drag me down, makes me murderous.

MUNSHIN

Nobody your age can go as far as you want to go . . . and carry a dame on his back.

EITEL

Only I can't brush her.

MUNSHIN

All right, then . . . go ahead, marry her.

EITEL

Marry her?

MUNSHIN

That's the answer.

EITEL

If I feel . . . back in prison with Elena, what do I solve by marriage?

MUNSHIN

There's one thing that's beautiful about this girl. She's not

119

a gold-digger. If you marry her, she'll feel you cared enough to give her your name. When you start talking about divorce, she'll be reasonable about money.

(Bell)

CHANGE TWO

(Elena enters)

MUNSHIN

You're exquisite, angel.

(She turns as if to answer)

Don't even answer.

(She makes an obscene gesture with her middle finger, looses one piercing whistle and exits)

Face it, Charley, there's no hope with Elena.

(Blackout—bell—many bells)

CHANGE ONE

(Lights come up. Eitel is all alone)

EITEL

You got an itch, go scratch it! . . . I saw magical possibilities for Elena and me. She was at the bottom . . . I was at the bottom. We could make something out of nothing. I must have been influenced by the movies I made. Because she is hopeless, socially she's hopeless—she blights my brain. And the worst of it is that I am still too ambitious, too snobbish, and too desirous of the power I destroyed for myself to be able to feel a little compassion for her cruelties, her stupidities, and her lack of grace—instead rage fires me, silent rage which eats at my finest nerves, and corrodes my talent. Yes, I am a rebel who loathes himself because he has done so little to change the monstrous world of lies, insanity, and the inch-by-inch killing of one another which is all we know—although we know better—and yet, rebel that I am, anarchist, false aristocrat, poet and surrogate-pimp, I cannot find it in myself to care to recover the love I loved her with for a few golden days, when I knew then and still know now that everything in her I detest, her voice, her manners, and her low uncharitable vulgar reactions to all that I would love dressed in wit, are the human cripplings that nine out of ten suffer because the world's so fear-filled, so hypocritical, so cowardly, so cruel, so sneaky and so bastard unjust, that we grow up all of us choked with venom, alert to murder each other inch-by-inch in order to stay alive ourselves. So I plot now to brush her, to brush this social cripple, by marriage, divorce, and all the fine icy steps between—and in my mind, giving up the joy that I was born to be one of the proud rebellious spirits of my generation, I begin to compose instead my song of the maggots—in the secret crawling corners of my brain I plot how to make a face-saving peace with the frightened bullies who would manage me, frightened bully that I must be.

(Dimout)

ACT TWO

CHANGE FORTY-FOUR

(The lights come up on the same set. Subtle—and easily removable— changes should be made to indicate we are now on the patio of an estate where a party is taking place. Eitel's first speech is thus off to one side of the set.

He and Elena, incidentally, are gotten up in proper style for a gala, and thus make a most handsome couple.)

EITEL

I've decided to go to Dorothea's party. You see, it is the first large party to which I've been invited in two years. Dorothea is, you may remember, Marion's mother, and so an old mistress. (Although in the time we were together she was not so much an old mistress as an electric harp.) Today, she's a gossip columnist, a vicious gossip columnist. She gets more vicious every year, and what she hates— that incoherent pottage she makes of sex, Communism, art, altruism and imaginative movies—comes I think out of her hatred for me, because in that female mind of hers she decided that if one artist deserted her, all art was evil.

(Elena enters.

Court-dance music strikes up. Eitel extends his hand gallantly into the darkness; Elena, taking it, walks into the light)

Yes, we're going to the party at Dorothea's.

(They exit)

125

CHANGE FORTY-THREE

(Marion saunters out. He is wearing evening clothes, and looks his best. Better than that. Cary Grant could not necessarily deliver the next speech with more charm.)

MARION

The sweetest pang in Eitel's breast is envy. He does not know. . . . Let me describe my mother's place. It is the showpiece of Desert D'Or. In the middle of this flat town in the flatlands of the desert my mother had a million-dollar hill built by bulldozers and put her home and her gardens and her patios and gazebos and pools and striped refreshment tents all up and down and over that hill, that monument to love which I call Bullshit Mountain. And the party tonight for three hundred of the best of the very worst people you could ever hope to meet takes place over that hill far away. Down here we are in naught but a tiny patio beneath a tiny *maison de joie* in a corner of the estate of BS Mountain, and only a few of the cognoscenti ever get down to here before returning to the party. But, hark, I hear my mother above the patio in her *maison de joie* and she is with the daddy of her dreams, Daddy Warbucks.

CHANGE FORTY-TWO

(This short scene discloses the real location of the platform from which Teppis has addressed his remarks to us all through the first act. A chaise-percé, his throne has feet of clay, for it serves . . . But watch.

126

*Lights on Teppis' throne high on
its platform above the action. Teppis rises and experimentally pulls
the thick velvet bell rope which
hangs by the side of the throne,
and is answered by the roar and
flush of some thunderous plumbing
filled with choir chimes and the
murmur of Victoria Falls. As the
lights brighten, we realize that the
carved throne is the centerpiece of
an elaborately decorated Renais-
sance bathroom of a sort which
may never have existed in the Ren-
aissance. Teppis turns to Dorothea.
who is in the room with him.)*

TEPPIS

I don't like this place. In my day, Dorothea, a bathroom
was a bathroom, it didn't look so good. You got the kind
of place people could end up living the rest of their lives
in, they could retire here and enjoy it. I got motion-picture
executives working for me, they don't get offices look as
good as this. A man my age having to hide at a party in
order to do a little business. It's ridiculous.

(Dimout)

CHANGE FORTY-ONE

MARION

As for myself—wait. I am up to something extraordinary
tonight. Revenge is a dish which people of taste eat cold.
Wait, your servant, Prince Marion.

*(At this point a few people show up
on the patio. Gusts of music come
from over the hill, and a laugh or*

127

*two, a woman seen in the shadows
who could be Zenlia. Then a panto-
mime between Munshin, Marion,
and Bobby, in which Bobby, as-
signed by Marion, walks off with
Munshin. Dorothea, having de-
scended to the patio and having regarded all this, now comes up behind Marion and speaks to him in
her deepest sweetest voice.)*

CHANGE FORTY

DOROTHEA

Tonight, I feel sentimental. I mourn the great gap between
you and me. Marion, I've been thinking of a time so long
ago when I was alone in my bedroom and weeping, and
you came in and stroked my cheek. You were only three
and a half but you said, "Don't cry, Mommie. Don't cry,
Mommie, because you're so pretty."

MARION

Sweetie, when I travel down memory lane, I remember the
smell of bitch, perfume and mummy all in one.

DOROTHEA

You have cruel blood.

MARION

I had a cruel daddy.

DOROTHEA

Your father was a prince from a very grand family.

MARION

Come on, Clytemnestra, you must have seen a play by
that old ding-dong Tennessee. My father was no devoted
prince, but some hard-ass who tooled you on a one-night
stand.

128

DOROTHEA

But you'll never know, will you, hateful?

MARION

I get closer to the truth by comparing your lies.

DOROTHEA

I love you. Won't you believe me?

MARION

Remember the stories you'd tell to everybody about how you saw me in a charity orphanage and loved my pretty face.

DOROTHEA

No one believed me. They knew you were my son.

MARION

But you told them I was an orphan anyway. You hadn't the guts to call me your own.

DOROTHEA

Believe that I love you.

MARION

Maybe I would like to believe you.

DOROTHEA

You can.

MARION

Can I? Would you give me what I asked for?

DOROTHEA

I always have.

MARION

Would you give me money?

DOROTHEA

Of course I would.

MARION

I don't want three hundred dollars. I think I may want three hundred thousand dollars.

129

DOROTHEA
What for?

MARION
I want to buy a plantation in Africa. Like Rimbaud, baby.

DOROTHEA
Three hundred thousand dollars. You *are* vicious.

MARION
Don't waste your adrenalin. It wrinkles the skin and arouses those aging odors no scent can cover.

DOROTHEA
You are killing me bit by bit.

> (*Lulu enters. It is, ideally, a magnificent entrance. Much subtle embrace between Dorothea and Lulu. It is obvious they are, to each other, all devoted.*)

CHANGE THIRTY-NINE

DOROTHEA
Lulu, I'd like you to meet my son.

LULU
But I know Marion. We had a dance together, Dorothea. It was a mad dance. And what made it so lovely is that your son can't really dance.

MARION
Go fix the flowers, fuck-face, was the king's reply.

> (*Marion exits*)

130

CHANGE THIRTY-EIGHT

DOROTHEA

Prison was tragic for him . . . Come, I'll get you a drink.

LULU and DOROTHEA
(Together)

Let's have a Small Martin.

LULU

The best Small Martin I ever had was in Saint Martin.

DOROTHEA

Drinking rum in Barbados, I lost a pair of white gloves.

(A young witch and an older witch have just established a bond)

CHANGE THIRTY-SEVEN

(Eitel and Elena enter. A pause as they all see each other)

LULU

Dorothea, do you know Charley?

DOROTHEA

Every time I see poor Charley Eitel at a party, people introduce us.

LULU

Once the two of you get together it will be a romance.

DOROTHEA

It was a romance.

ELENA

It's a very nice party I think. I mean up there. It's nice on the hill.

131

(Lulu giggles and exits. It is the cruellest giggle of the night. And the most successful exit.)

DOROTHEA
(To Elena)
Don't let a thing get you down, sweetie pie.

CHANGE THIRTY-SIX

DOROTHEA
(Circling her)
A nice restful girl like this.

(Elena starts to move away.

To Elena)
You put me in mind of how my good dear friend the Senator would feel. He always says he's an admirer of attractive women. What a shame he isn't here tonight.

EITEL
Why isn't he?

DOROTHEA
Oh, he would have loved to be here, but he's visiting the President.

EITEL
May he fall off a horse.

DOROTHEA
Listen, you old hambone, you have the idea we want to persecute you. Not true. But you said some pretty potent things. It left a bad taste with the press. I've had to work overtime to make a few people realize your case ought to be reconsidered. Now I have a decent offer for you. Charles Francis, you can't stop a man who has a redhead working for him. This is what she just might be authorized to propose. You get up before a closed session of the Committee

132

and say you're sorry. Then you give us a dozen names, no more.

EITEL

Do I make up the names or do you spell them for me?

DOROTHEA

The names you give will be old ones. So you won't hurt a soul.

EITEL

I'm not certain I feel ready for the kiss.

DOROTHEA

Don't stay on tiptoe too long.

EITEL

(There is the hint of a flaw in his voice)

I won't be able to come back unless I crawl on my belly?

DOROTHEA

We do want you, but if it must be on your belly, why yes, Charley, by all means there.

ELENA

What?

DOROTHEA

Ooo la la. I shouldn't talk this way in front of a third party.

(To Elena)

Gardez ton nez, cherie, which is French for keep your nose clean, luscious.

(She exits)

CHANGE THIRTY-FIVE

ELENA

How could you stand there and listen to her?

EITEL

What do you want me to do, knock her down?

ELENA

She insulted you and then she insulted me. Let's leave this party.

EITEL

No, not yet.

ELENA

Why not?

EITEL

Because coming to this party turned on a switch in my dear old burned-out brain and I don't want to turn it off so soon.

ELENA

You're up to something that's no good at all. I can feel it.

EITEL

Darling, I want to go back and make films. Simple as that. It eats at me like the dream of a woman in jail. But I don't choose to give in to them. Will you trust me?

ELENA

I don't know. I think you might be feeling sick looking at them with all their money.

EITEL

Listen, pet, I haven't taken the couple of punches I've taken in my little life in order to be talked to in this sprightly fashion by you. If you're afraid of the party, don't feel obliged to provoke me.

134

ELENA

Afraid?

EITEL

Afraid!

ELENA

That did it. Charley, stay away from me for awhile, will you? I've waited years to get to a party like this.

EITEL

Bless you. Have a ball.

ELENA

That's the way to do it.

(They separate in opposite directions)

CHANGE THIRTY-FOUR

(Lights up on Teppis. Teddy Pope has just entered.)

TEDDY

Sorry to get here so late, Mr. Teppis, but I just found your message ten minutes ago, when I arrived at my hotel after a quiet evening with some friends.

TEPPIS

Quiet. I'm glad it was quiet. I know a young fellow like you with the world at his feet . . . there's a lot of times he don't want to get married. "Why should I get married?" he says to himself. "What's in it for me?" Teddy, I'll tell you, there's a lot in it for you. Just think. The whole world is in a straitjacket so it says, "You over there, you get in a straitjacket, too." Know why? The world hates a bachelor, he's not popular. The stories you hear, ninety-nine percent of the time unfounded, but I'd be ashamed, I couldn't look you in the eye to tell you the kind of stories

I have to listen to. I hear a story like that, I let them have it. "Don't tell me that kind of filth about Teddy," I say. "I don't want to hear it. If the boy don't want to get married, it got nothing to do with all those dirty stories you tell me. Period!" That's confidence. Teddy, should I put that confidence in you? Don't answer. I've had my confidence rewarded already. That picture of you and Lulu holding hands in Desert D'Or. It's one of the most beautiful, impressive, touching things I've ever seen. Lulu's wearing her heart on her sleeve. She's a fine American-type girl of real American stock. Such a woman is a gift of God.

TEDDY

Mr. Teppis—that's a publicity picture.

TEPPIS

Stop! You're a stubborn boy. I don't want to hear your ideas. Why do you act so cockeyed when you know you want a man like myself to set you straight?

TEDDY
(In a quiet voice)
You know very well I'm a homosexual.

TEPPIS
(Screams)
I didn't hear it. I didn't hear it.

TEDDY

That's the way I am . . .

(Mutters)

What is, is.

TEPPIS

Philosophy?

(Shouts)

If a man sits in shit, he don't know enough to get out of it?

TEDDY

Mr. Teppis, don't you have a big enough heart to understand my feelings?

136

TEPPIS

You're the most ungrateful boy I ever knew. What do you think, sex, it's the whole world?

TEDDY

Let me try to say . . .

TEPPIS

Lulu, that's what you got to say. You're a coward. You got a chip against society. You should love society, with all it's done for you. I love society. I respect it. Teddy, you're a sick boy, but you and me can lick this thing together.

(Holds up his fist for our delectation as the BLACKOUT hits)

CHANGE THIRTY-THREE

(Back to the patio. Elena discovers herself not quite alone. Marion at one end, a strange and attractive couple at the other)

ELENA

You're Don Beda, aren't you?

BEDA

You know my name?

ELENA

Charley told me about you once.

ZENLIA
(In a beautiful English accent)
Oh yes? What did he say about my husband?

ELENA
(Half uncomfortably, half boldly)
He didn't say it, but I got the feeling you like animals as much as women.

BEDA

I assure you, my dear, I'm much more dreadful than that.

ZENLIA
(To Elena)

I know this is on the treacly side, but you remind me of my cousin . . . She has rather an intense grace.

ELENA
(In a comic English accent)

Well, I have rather an intense disgrace.

(All four laugh)

BEDA

My wife is trying to distract me from saying that I find you as splendid as wine.

ZENLIA

A divine wine.

ELENA

Thanks. Thanks a lot.

BEDA

You were born to be the center of attraction in a warm room with cruel eyes upon you.

ELENA

Well that's not so bad. I was worried we were going to have a romance.

ZENLIA

My poor husband. He's too good, you see. I always say that a woman can never fall in love with a man who's too marvelous in bed.

ELENA

What do you people eat for breakfast?

BEDA

One vanishes at dawn.

ELENA
(Laughs)

138

Say, let's get together. I haven't had a good nightmare in years.

(She walks away from them. Mar-
ion applauds, fingertips mocking
fingertips.)

CHANGE THIRTY-TWO

BEDA

What do you think?

ZENLIA

We may have lost her. She's the sort of a girl who won't think you're serious unless you're altogether solemn. Still, excelsior, lip, toot! and do your best, angel, to work up a scrumptious fuck.

BEDA

I'm going to make solemn sounds to Elena.

(Zenlia extends her hand for Mar-
ion's kiss. As he strolls by, Beda
casually lifts Marion's free hand to
his lips and moves on.)

CHANGE THIRTY-ONE

MARION

If you nip me the wrong way, I'll break your jaw.

ZENLIA

Let's go, you maniac.

(Marion and Zenlia exit as the lights
shift)

CHANGE THIRTY

TEDDY

Mr. Teppis, I'd like to have children and a wife, but it's still a psychological impossibility.

TEPPIS

Teddy, don't make up your mind ahead of time that you personally aren't able to boff a beautiful sexy girl like Lulu. Do I have to be there to help you? I'm telling you, you can.

(Makes a move to signify the interview is over)

Now, Teddy, nobody is forcing you into anything. If you said yes this very minute, I would still say, "Teddy, sleep on it." Could anybody claim I was trying to push you into a single thing?

TEDDY

Who would dare?

TEPPIS

You're right. I don't force people. Never. I talk things over with them.

CHANGE TWENTY-NINE

(On the stairs which lead from the maison de joie *to the patio)*

TEDDY

What I would like is for something to happen where I could be true to myself.

140

CHANGE TWENTY-EIGHT

(Nobody gets away from Teppis this easily)

TEPPIS

Some day, Teddy, you're going to say, "God bless you, H.T."

(On the wake of Teddy's exit)

Fagela momser!

CHANGE TWENTY-SEVEN

(The patio.

Lulu and Eitel enter separately)

LULU

Charley, are you in the mood to listen? I have the feeling that you're the only one alive who can understand me, right now.

EITEL

Why me?

LULU

Because, Charles, you hurt me and I've always thought it's the people who can hurt you the most who understand you the best.

EITEL

Lulu, I just might know what you mean.

LULU

I'm in love again.

EITEL

Not with Tony Tanner?

LULU

I'm the only one who understands a certain side of Tony.

EITEL

Yes, you are in love.

LULU

I'm practically positive.

EITEL

You must want me to kill it for you.

LULU

You're drunk. The weird thing is I don't think Tony is in love with me.

> *(They are, however, talking in reality of other things, of . . . of animal magnetism)*

What are you thinking?

EITEL

I was just deciding it's impossible to remember what an ex-wife's body looks like.

LULU

Don't you remember?

EITEL

Certain visions are engraved.

LULU

Charles, I think you're very attractive tonight but I want to remain faithful to Tony.

> *(Elena enters. They do not see her just yet.)*

EITEL

Balls.

LULU
You're mean.

CHANGE TWENTY-SIX

ELENA

I want to go home now . . . you don't have to come.

LULU

Why don't you stay, Charley? You have permission.

EITEL

Let's all have a drink.

LULU

Uh-uh.

EITEL

Goodnight, Lulu.

(Lulu exits)

CHANGE TWENTY-FIVE

ELENA

You're a coward . . . you wanted to go away with Lulu and
I ruined it.

(In triumph)

I ruined it.

EITEL

You didn't ruin anything.

ELENA
*(Her face is furious with the effort
not to cry)*

Why do you lie to me this way?

EITEL

It's absurd, Elena . . . what if I did feel a minute's something-or-other for Lulu? I didn't mean it. We're here . . . together, aren't we?

ELENA

I'll tell you something. That friend of yours, that disgusting man, Don Beda, asked me to go home with him and his wife. And he said things to me . . . he thinks I'm dirt. Well, maybe I am dirt. I wanted to go with him . . . So, if you want to have your fun, don't think I'm the one who's stopping you, because I can have my fun, too. Want to go to an orgy, Charley?

EITEL

My poor baby.

(It is not really as bad as it sounds. He is not disapproving of her suggestion because it offends his morals—rather it offends his sense of how far away they are from each other the moment they are not close together. Besides, he believes she must be in deep pain to say this.)

ELENA
(Shouts)

I hate you!

CHANGE TWENTY-FOUR

(Eitel approaches her)

ELENA

Go away.

EITEL

I want us to be married. I've ruined everything I've touched. But you must know that I care about you. I can't stand

144

the thought of hurting you . . . I know how much you want to be married, because you feel nobody cares about you. I want to show you that I do.

ELENA

You have no respect for me.

EITEL

But I have so much respect, can't you see?

ELENA

Don't you understand? You asked me in such a way I'd have to spit on myself to say yes. You want me to say no and set you free.

(*He looks away—he is surprisingly close to the need to weep*)

Cheer up, Charley, it's really not so bad—

(*A sad little wisdom appears*)

I can always find another man.

(*Beda, Marion and Zenlia enter*)

CHANGE TWENTY-THREE

(*Beda comes out in search of Eitel and Elena. Seeing them, he begins to hum an operatic air. They separate slowly.*)

BEDA

Charley, Zenlia and I are going over to Marion's place and, *sans façons,* we'd like you to come too.

ELENA

(*Recovering her composure first— a little warily*)

What are we all supposed to do?

145

BEDA

You're not signing a contract to do anything, my dear. Get into your car. We'll be waiting for you at the turn of the road.

ELENA
(Obliquely)
Don, is it true Zenlia used to be friends with that oily king?

BEDA

Not oily, my dear. He owns oil. Why, the king is charming.

> *(Beda, Marion and Zenlia exit—it is the most suggestive exit of the night)*

CHANGE TWENTY-TWO

ELENA

I think we're out of our class.

EITEL

But you're willing to go . . .

ELENA

Well, we know where we stand, champ.

EITEL

I don't want to go.

ELENA

I do.

EITEL

You may have to go alone.

ELENA

You're afraid to go.

EITEL

Afraid! I took a wife away from Don Beda once.

Bravo! Whatever did happen to her?

> *(Beda—all antennae out—the director need not take this literally—returns for Elena. She exits with Beda.)*

CHANGE TWENTY-ONE

> *(Lulu passes Eitel on the patio. He seizes her and embraces her.)*

LULU

You're out of control.

EITEL

I want you. I want to go away with you. I stayed at this party to go away with you.

LULU

You're starting to press, Charley, and it's dull. Do you really think I want your bulk back again on me when all I can think of is a stud, Charley, as young and marvelous as Tony. Sit down for awhile Daddy-O. Get your second wind.

> *(Exits.*
>
> *Dorothea enters)*

DOROTHEA

You're too old, Charley, and much too sweet for all of this.

> *(Eitel exits in the direction Elena has taken)*

147

CHANGE TWENTY

(Tony and Lulu enter)

LULU

What are they getting ready to do?

DOROTHEA

The orgy bit.

(Exits)

LULU

Would you like to?

TONY

Are you out of your snake skin? I don't put you up for nobody's grabs.

LULU

Oh well, I wouldn't go. I wouldn't dare. I think of things like raids.

TEPPIS
(From upstairs)

LoooooLooooo!

(Lulu and Tony exit at a great rate)

CHANGE NINETEEN

(Sergius has witnessed the last of this)

SERGIUS

Do you know, there are times when I miss the Air Force. It has finally gotten through that hard head of mine that

148

Lulu has given me the brush. Call me Cannonball. Look, two weeks ago I told Lulu a little too much about me and I could see her take a chill. She said, "It's hard enough to make a movie without you telling me stories like that."

> *(Lulu returns with Tony and runs into Sergius)*
>
> **TEPPIS**
> *(From upstairs)*

LOOOOLOOO!

> *(Lulu attempts to leave but is held by)*

LOOOOOLOOOOO!

> *(She goes upstairs)*

CHANGE EIGHTEEN

TEPPIS
I love a girl like you. You bring sunshine into this room.

LULU
I love you too, Mr. T.

> *(Teppis guides her to the chair in which Teddy had been sitting, and from a drawer in a vanity table takes out a bottle of whiskey and drops some ice cubes into a glass)*

I'm not drinking tonight.

TEPPIS
Nonsense. I know you, sweetie. I don't want you thinking you got to take a drink behind my back.

LULU
You're the only man who understands me, H.T.

Nobody can understand you. Know why? You're a great
woman. Fire, spirit, charm! Those are the sort of things
you have. Take a drink. You've earned the right to do anything you want.

LULU

Except to disagree with you, H.T.

TEPPIS

I love you. You got impetuosity. Know my personal opinion of Lulu Meyers? Lulu Meyers is the greatest actress
in this country, and this country's got the greatest actors
in the whole world.

LULU

You're the greatest actor in the world, H.T.

TEPPIS

I take it as a compliment. But you're wrong, Lulu, I can't
act. I'm too sincere. You know what eats my heart out?
It's that I'm not the American public. If I was the American public, I'd make you Number One on the Bimmler Rat-
ings. Know what you are now?

LULU

Seventeen, isn't it, Mr. T.?

TEPPIS

Seventeen. Can you believe it? There are sixteen actors in
this country the American public buys ahead of you. Last
year you were six. Number Six.

LULU

Maybe I'm a has-been.

TEPPIS

Lulu, for a remark like that, I ought to take you up over
my knee and spank you. Lulu, listen to me; the trouble is
you're weak publicity-wise.

LULU

I've got the best press agent in the country.

TEPPIS

You think you can buy publicity? Good publicity is a gift of God. It's psychology.

> *(One small insight may be permitted here into Teppis' absolute logic: Psychology is what? Why, it is the ability to understand others and so control them. Therefore psychology equals power. Power is a gift of God, Q.E.D. Let no one say Teppis is illogical.)*

The public wants to see a woman they can respect. A royal couple, the Number One married lovers of America. That's true psychology.

LULU

H.T., you should have been a marriage broker.

TEPPIS

I'll tell you something. If you could be married to the right kind of boy, to a star, let's say, with a Seven Bimmler, a Nine Bimmler, you think you'd come up with a Bimmler the average between the two of you? You wouldn't. You'd end up with the two highest Bimmlers in America, and America is the world, that's where you'd be.

(Blows a kiss at Lulu)

I got something on my mind that's going to stun you. Want to know who I think you should marry?

LULU

I can never guess what you think, Mr. Teppis.

TEPPIS

Guess. Go ahead, guess.

LULU

Tony Tanner.

TEPPIS

Tony Tanner? Lulu, I'm ashamed of you. I looked *up* his Bimmler myself. One hundred eighty-nine, that's what a

151

nobody he is. I got somebody better. Don't say a word; sleep on it . . . Teddy Pope, what do you say?

LULU

H.T., I feel as if things can never be the same between us.

TEPPIS

Sit down, I'll tell you something. I got no desire to hide it from you. Teddy Pope is a homosexual. It makes you wonder. Could H.T. be the kind of man who gets down on his hands and knees to beg a beautiful girl like you to marry a faggola?

LULU

You couldn't. You're too respectable.

TEPPIS

Let's not get off the sidetrack. Answer me one question as honest as you can. Do you admit that to be married to Teddy Pope wouldn't that be the biggest benefit you could bestow on yourself publicity-wise? The Number One couple of America. Say I'm right.

LULU

I don't like Teddy.

TEPPIS

Teddy Pope is the man for you. He's delicate and sensitive. There's a lot for an actress to learn from him about the subtleties of human nature. Lulu, you're the woman who could straighten him out, and then he'd worship the ground you walk on.

LULU

I hate you, H.T.

TEPPIS

Hate me! You love me! That's why you hate to listen to me. Think of the respect people would have if you could make a man out of Teddy Pope.

LULU

H.T., I want to get married . . . I want to love just one

152

man and have a beautiful relationship and be a credit to
the industry.

TEPPIS

That's the ticket, Lulu.

LULU

But if I marry Teddy, I'll become promiscuous.

TEPPIS

Lulu, you could never be promiscuous. You're too fine.
Suppose at the very worst that when you're married to
Teddy, there should be a fellow or two that you would
like and admire and diddle around with. I don't advise it,
but it happens, and you know what? The world don't stop
moving.

LULU

Diddle around with. H.T., that's an immoral proposal . . .
I'm ashamed of you.

TEPPIS

Ashamed of me? You said the wrong thing then. There are
a lot of high executives in this studio who are fed up with
you. Believe me, Lulu, as God is looking into this room,
you've made enemies, hundreds of enemies.

LULU

I'm amazed you should stoop to intimidate me.

TEPPIS

Don't fool me . . . You're scared stiff! Lulu, be my witness, don't even answer me right away. Would you turn
H.T. down on the only favor he ever asked of you?

LULU

Oh, Mr. Teppis, I love you.

TEPPIS

Would you marry Teddy Pope?

LULU

I want to marry Teddy Pope after the way you explained
it, Mr. Teppis.

TEPPIS

I don't want to talk you into it.

LULU

I'd marry Teddy in a minute now . . . But I can't.

TEPPIS

Of course you can . . . Why not?

LULU

'Cause I married Tony Tanner this morning.

>*(The lights go out. In the darkness
>Teppis roars like a bull.)*

TEPPIS

God, how could *You* do this to *Me?*

LULU
(Still in the dark)
Mr. Teppis, would you like a glass of water?

TEPPIS

Drop dead. I wouldn't even look at your grave.

>*(A trembling fit of lights. Full lights.
>Munshin enters)*

MUNSHIN

When are the wedding bells?

>*(Teppis cannot speak to Munshin.
>He waves one maddened limb [his
>finger] at Lulu)*

TEPPIS

Out of here. You're a common whoor.

LULU

Ohh.

(She runs)

MUNSHIN

Oy, Jesus.

154

TEPPIS
(After Lulu)

Come back here.

MUNSHIN

Come back here.

(Lulu is gone)

TEPPIS
(To Munshin)

Shut up.

MUNSHIN
(After a nonexistent Lulu)

Shut up.

(Night falls mercifully on the scene. A quick Blackout)

CHANGE SEVENTEEN

SERGIUS

Did you know I was in a mental bin? Yeah. I came here, better believe it, because these people who manufacture images fascinated me. I mean, imagination can be more real than reality. I had the feeling I could find my brain right here.

CHANGE SIXTEEN

(Lights up again on Munshin and Teppis)

TEPPIS

That Teddy Pope. A degraded homosexual. I had him twisted into a pretzel.

MUNSHIN

You're right, H.T.

TEPPIS

I'm nauseous. A dime-a-dozen comedian, a coarse person like Tony Tanner. I hate coarse people. Isn't there any class left in the world?

MUNSHIN

You're the class, H.T.

TEPPIS

Shut up! I let you marry my only daughter. I made you my executive assistant. I know you, Collie, you'll cut my throat someday. Do you hear me? I know your tricks!

MUNSHIN

H.T., a genius like you will turn this catastrophe into something catatonic.

TEPPIS

My indigestion is upset.

MUNSHIN

I've learned everything from you, H.T. Teddy is through. You'll pick up the newspaper someday and Teddy will be on the front page for hanging roses in the men's room at the Y.

TEPPIS

You got a disgusting imagination.

156

I'm a realist. So are you, H.T. No other studio could make a nickel handling Tony, but your genius will do it. Think of the publicity. Tony Tanner the cocky kid who stole Atom Bomb Lulu Meyers right from under a big lover type like Teddy Pope. You've done it again, H.T.

TEPPIS

Don't give me compliments. My indigestion is upset.

MUNSHIN

The doctor told me you got to lower your nervous tension.

TEPPIS

You're my son-in-law and you're a pimp. If it weren't for my daughter, I'd fire you.

MUNSHIN

I've got a sweet kid for you, H.T. She'll button her lip tight as a virgin's bun.

TEPPIS

You're a foul-mouthed individual. You get the hell out, Collie. You think a man can break the laws of society? Those laws are for a purpose. Every time you send up a girl I don't even want to see her again. I refuse to sleep with her.

(Munshin makes a signal. Bobby enters)

MUNSHIN

Nobody works the way you do, H.T.

(He exits)

CHANGE FIFTEEN

TEPPIS
(To Bobby)
Come here, sweetie . . . don't you worry, sweetie . . .

(She kneels before him.

To the world at large)

There's a monster in the human heart.

CHANGE FOURTEEN

SERGIUS

There's nothing like being up early. In the air at four in the morning, coffee on your tongue. Our wing man always used to wiggle his plane like a cooch dancer, and soon we were all laughing and wiggling our tails, cause he was a good crazy guy, you know. Sometimes on tactical missions we would lay fire bombs into Oriental villages. I didn't like that particularly, but I would be busy with technique, and I would dive my plane and release my payload into my part of the pattern. I hardly thought of it any other way. From the air a city in flames is not a bad sight. One morning I came back from such a mission and went into Officers' Mess for lunch. We were stationed at an airfield near Tokyo, and one of the Japanese KP's, a fifteen-year-old boy, had just burned his arm in a kettle of spilled soup. Like most Orientals he was durable, and so he served the dishes with one hand, his burned arm held behind him, while the sweat stood out on his nose, and he bobbed his head in

158

little shakes because he was disturbing our service. I could not take my eyes from the burn; it ran from the elbow to the shoulder and the skin had turned to blisters. After lunch I took the Jap aside and asked the cooks for tannic acid ointment. There wasn't any in the kitchen so I told them to boil tea and put compresses on his arm. Suddenly I realized that two hours ago I had been setting fire to a dozen people, or two dozen, or had it been a hundred? Well, now I began to see the other side of it. You see, we were dropping jellied gasoline—a drop on a man and the man is the fire, fire hot enough to melt your skull.

(As Sergius speaks, the orgiasts— Beda, Zenlia, Marion and Elena— pass by him along the patio, which is all but dark, and take up their posts in some part of the stage or theatre not occupied until now. Eitel, in a short while, will join them. Sergius is, of course, separated by lights and position from the others.)

CHANGE THIRTEEN

ZENLIA

Green fire. The only fire I like is green fire.

BEDA

As you have gathered, my hobby is to cultivate the orgy —its care, creation and preservation. That, little children,

159

is the only platform still protecting me from the pit of total boredom.

ZENLIA

Experience teaches a world of wonders. One learns, for example, that there are two kinds of monarchs. Those who eat their mistresses' dire flop, and those who don't. The second variety is not easy to live with. They know nothing of perfume.

MARION

Sex is a form of speech and I speak to many. Some conversations give me pleasure more than others. But if ever a conversation came to me which gave promise of going forever, I would remain under the spell of such a dialogue.

ELENA

I am the center of attention. The hole at the center of my soul fills with honey.

EITEL

The director is the voyeur and the sculptor and the match which strikes the flame. Now I am only the voyeur. I direct nothing. I take photographs on my retina of the dimensions of my shame.

SERGIUS

I used to wonder what the corpses looked like. We had press agents. To give us box-office, I suppose. We'd fly a group mission and they'd give it a name. Operation Castanet or Punchbowl or Red-hot Mama. Every time I'd go out on a flight, I'd yell when I dropped the bombs, "I enjoy it. I enjoy the fire," I'd yell and I did. I'd come back and I'd cut a swath through the Geisha houses. Once I had five girls in one night. "I'm good for you, baby,"

160

I would tell them. "I got the cruelty
to make you happy."

ZENLIA

Asparagus and avocado. I lay them down and pick them
up. I nibble and I lick. I love to run my hands through
watercress and down steel wool and silk. There is no end
to the wonder of hair? From where can it come? To whom
does it belong?

*(Elena laughs. It is a long sensuous
laugh, full of ripples, and languors,
and turnings which give hint of delight.)*

EITEL

Love me? You love everything. A gorilla, a hyena, a four-
eyed horse. You love me, yes, you do. Why you can
give your yelps and yowls to any two-bit dog.

SERGIUS

Then it would begin. I'd be saw-
ing away on some slut and I'd close
my eyes to enjoy it, and man, I'd
see a butcher shop. Because flesh
is raw in the real world. Nothing
but flesh comes into my mind—
bursting flesh, rotting flesh, flesh
hung on spikes in butcher stalls,
flesh burning, flesh gone to blood.
One day I felt as if a meat cleaver
went right through my brain and
I was in the hospital. Or at least
that is the way I remember it!

ELENA

I tried to commit suicide the day Collie told me he was
tearing it. I sat in that cheap hotel room he had rented
for me and I started to drink—alone—and I drank until
the room wouldn't stand still. I thought I was going to die
if the room didn't stop moving. "Collie," I kept saying,
"you and me were just an old sewer."

161

(On this speech, Eitel leaves the others, and takes a slow overburdened walk back to his favorite seat on the set, the director's chair)

MARION
Mire the body in offal. So the soul may relinquish its heart.

BEDA
The night is in the saddle of the hills. The hours pass. Look—the night has drained the blood from one.

ZENLIA
On with the lights—I want to see the face of the sweet little beasts who make love to me.

MARION
Eitel has come home. The wounded always return to the place where they first knew the hunter held their heart in his eye.

SERGIUS
I was in the hospital and for the first time in my life I had to think. And that is a terrible demand to make of a native-born American like me.

(As Sergius is speaking these last words, Marion, Zenlia and Beda have been filing off. The light goes out on Sergius, and comes up. In the half dark, the few modifications necessary to bring the set back from the patio to Eitel's ranch house have been taken. We are back, yes, at the ranch again. So Elena steps directly from this last scene into the next, from the orgy—if you permit this—to the home.)

CHANGE TWELVE

ELENA

Love, Charley—I love you.

EITEL

Don't come near me.

ELENA

Charley, I love you.

EITEL

Love, Elena? Love is just a big noise.

ELENA

Yes, I love you. But I don't love you completely. You're too greedy. You don't really want me and yet you want every last bit of me. Well, let me tell you . . . maybe I want other rhythms in my body besides yours.

EITEL

I'll never touch you again.

ELENA

Oh, lover, touch me.

(She reaches for him but he moves away)

Oh, Charley, don't you see, they had to have me, I was the center of attention. Oh, come here, love, come to me.

(He does not move)

Listen, I don't love you. I never loved anybody. I'm too conceited. So don't feel guilty. You don't owe me nothing.

EITEL

You bitch, you worship stupidity as if it were your patron saint.

163

ELENA

Want to know how stupid I am? I tried to commit suicide the day Collie told me he was tearing it. Yes. "Collie," I kept saying, "you and me were just an old sewer."

EITEL

Shut your foul mouth.

ELENA

I'm just getting started, Charley boy. How do you like my crude manners, hey, sweetheart? Say listen. When Collie came to my room, I saw the executive in him, magnificent, daddy, he said, "Hello," and slapped me a few times, and asked, "Where's the pill bottle?" and when he saw it, he began to laugh, and he said, "You idiot, those aren't sleeping pills, those are just bromides and No-Doz." and he began to jazz me right there and then.

(Eitel starts to leave)

No, you listen to every last bit of this . . . I never told you this, but Collie was pretty good, and I always used to act it was great with him, but of course I used to act with all of them until the night I met you . . .

(Eitel looks at her in disbelief)

. . . except that's a lie, you're right, Charley, because that night with Collie, the night before you, I let go, I mean I really let go—I thought I was in ether or something—what poison I was getting out of me, and the funny thing was that I couldn't have cared less about Collie, why we even had a talk afterward and he decided he would see me for a night every now and then, and he would pay me. Dig, Charley boy?

EITEL

Are you done?

ELENA

Can't you take it?

EITEL

I can take it.

164

I mean consider my delicate ladylike elegant feelings. I mean, this great jazz with Collie, and the moment he's done, he's got to make it clear that tomorrow you are coming over, you Charley, my first john, my bathroom—Collie is setting me up in business—you sons of bitches—and you know what?—I was fantastically excited, I don't know if it was you or the situation or because I was finally nothing but a whore, but it was crazy with you, Charley, it was all the way out. And in the morning I realized you didn't think of me as a call girl. You didn't know. You were cornering me into a love affair, and don't think I didn't want it with you, except I knew I could eat up the whole world if only I wasn't afraid to live and be free.

(Eitel nods)

Yes, Charley, as of now I am free and it's frightening. Oh, Charley boy, it's terrifying as hell. Because women, Charley, weren't born to be free, they were born to have babies, I suppose, and I am getting weird and wild and really scared inside because it's too good, Charley, I mean like tonight I got too much from everybody—Wow! Oh, my God, Charley, I've gone too far—I keep telling myself, "You can't cheat life," and I feel like I can, I mean, Charley, let's cut the crap—you get on the telephone and get me a taxi because I'm going over to live with Marion— Yes, there is where I should be—with Marion—he asked me tonight, yes, you cheap cowardly son of a bitch, I'm taking off. Listen, Charley, I'm going up and up, I need a lot of men, that's the only way a bitch like me can learn anything, from men, you little idiots, you're so pleased with yourselves when you're done, well, kiss off and thanks, because now I have the key and it's going to unlock a few doors—it must be because I have a hole eating away in me—if that cold bitch Zenlia can get herself a king, I ought to rate an emperor, because I was born to be a queen, oh God, that's all that can save me—Do you have anything to answer now?

EITEL
(Eitel goes up to her. He smiles

165

*ambiguously. We do not know if
he will embrace her or turn away.
And she moves toward him on the
hint. He smiles again.)*

Go peddle your papers, kid.

ELENA
*(With the cry of a wounded ani-
mal)*

Yes, yes. Good-bye, Charley.

(She exits)

CHANGE ELEVEN

(Eitel is alone)

EITEL
Where, in what cemetery of the heavens, do the tender
words of lovers rest when they love no more?

CHANGE TEN

*(Eitel is still alone. From behind
him, up on the platform where Teppis has remained all night, comes
the old producer's voice. Eitel is
hearing him in a kind of hallucination whose quality is suggested by
the lights.)*

TEPPIS
I like you, you miserable crook, I want you back.

EITEL
You'll have to break something first.

166

TEPPIS

In you, I'll break it.

EITEL

I miss you, Herman.

TEPPIS

I could cry when I think you ain't here to play me the insults. Go to hell, Eitel. I believe in God. He's picked on me.

EITEL

Why you?

TEPPIS

Because He's like me, an old man who knows what it's all about, and could throw up it's such a mess. Excuse me. I believe He gives His vote to the man who wins.

EITEL

Amen.

> (*Teppis descends the stairs and sits down next to Eitel. The illusion of hallucination must not, however, be dispelled.*)

TEPPIS

Eitel, why do I bother? It can't be the money.

EITEL

Herman, you can't be happy until you touch every last button on the machine.

TEPPIS

Say something nice to me. I've had a miserable night.

EITEL

I can't help it, you're not a very nice old man.

TEPPIS
(*Begins to weep*)

You. You were the only one I cared about. You never fit in. You had class.

EITEL

(Not without tenderness)

It's all changing, old pirate. Soon they'll make movies with electronic machines and you'll be gone.

TEPPIS

You like me a little.

EITEL

I don't like anybody anymore.

TEPPIS

Then you'll be back with me.

EITEL

I think that what I'll do is never make another picture. I'll take silence.

TEPPIS

You can't. You're a whore. You think a whore can stay alone in a room?

EITEL

We're all whores, sir.

TEPPIS

Leave the women out of it.

EITEL

Oh, the women. They *are* whores.

TEPPIS

Nobody talks about women that way in my presence.

(Slaps Eitel)

Listen, you bum, I've given to charity all my life.

EITEL

You'll die of cancer.

TEPPIS

Then society, God bless it, goes with me.

> *(Exit Teppis. Eitel is left alone in the wreckage of the patio.*

*Dorothea speaks from the platform
where we first saw her at the beginning of the act—it is still another part of the hallucination.)*

DOROTHEA
(Vaguely)

You're too old, Charley, you're too sweet for all of this.

*(Dorothea wanders off. Eitel is
alone. Lights fade)*

CHANGE NINE

*(A single spot on Marion. The light
flickers with a hint of lightning or
some kind of distant explosion.
Marion turns full circle, scanning
the horizon.)*

MARION

It seems they are testing another atom bomb tonight.

*(Wild laugh from Elena. She is dial-
ing the phone.)*

EITEL

Hello? . . . Hello? . . . Who is it? . . . Elena? . . . Is it
you? . . . Hello? . . . Hello!

(Elena hangs up)

ELENA

It seems like my old pal Charley is back in town.

MARION

There you are, with your hard wop heart, and yet you
loved him.

ELENA

What would you know?

169

MARION

You really loved him. No wonder you never got around to telling Eitel about some of the men and boys you did to get a two-bit booking in a nightclub.

ELENA

Not as many as you think. Believe it or not, I had my pride.

MARION

Like your old pal, Charley.

ELENA

Lay off him.

MARION

You think he's all right?

ELENA

I don't want to talk about it.

MARION

See the newspapers today?

ELENA

I don't read the newspapers.

MARION

You're a dull broad.

ELENA

Your friend, Don Beda, doesn't think I'm so dull. Know what I mean?

MARION
(Takes a clipping from his pocket)
"It has taken me years of wasted and misplaced effort"—dig, Elena—*"misplaced effort,* to recognize the useful and patriotic function of the Committee, and I testify today without duress, proud to be able to contribute my share to the defense of this country against all infiltration and subversion." That's us, honey.

ELENA

He didn't write it. Somebody gave it to him to sign.

170

MARION
(Laughs)

They must have peeled Eitel inch by inch.

ELENA

Knock off, will you?

MARION
(Reading)

"I can only add that it is the duty of every citizen to aid the Committee in its work with whatever knowledge he may possess."

ELENA
(Interrupting)

It bores me.

MARION

You have no inner life.

ELENA

I don't. Don't I know I don't.

MARION

You certainly don't.

ELENA

Why don't you make me a call-girl?

MARION

You couldn't make it as a call-girl.

ELENA

I could be a very good call-girl.

MARION

When one gets to know you well, you're raw meat. You lack class.

ELENA

All right, make me a prostitute.

MARION

Let's get married.

ELENA

I'd never marry you.

MARION

Dearest—what if I'm the one who won't marry you?

ELENA

I want to be a prostitute.

MARION

I don't touch prostitutes . . . I could send you to a friend, though. He has a job where you could work half in a whorehouse.

ELENA

What does half in a whorehouse mean?

MARION

It means in a whorehouse . . . on the Mexican border.

ELENA

I won't do that.

MARION

Are you a snob, doctor? Think of all the poor creeps down there and how they're crawling for you.

ELENA

I'm getting out.

MARION

Get out.

ELENA

I'll go.

MARION

Can you find the door?

ELENA

I'd like to kill myself.

MARION

You haven't got the guts.

172

ELENA
Don't taunt me. I could do it.

MARION
(Takes out a small bottle)
I've been saving these for myself. They're like sleeping pills. Except that two is enough. Two capsules. But it's enough.

ELENA
You think I won't?

MARION
I think you'll look at them.

ELENA
How long have you had those pills?

MARION
I put them in my pocket today.

ELENA
But when did you begin to think of having them . . . for me?

MARION
Lying next to you in bed. The first time. When you were just beginning to go with Eitel.

(Tenderly)

I said to myself, "This child is the material out of which suicides are made."

ELENA
You knew.

MARION
My mind never stops. I'm always hearing the words of my will. My will said to me, "You can make her kill herself."

ELENA
Why?

MARION
You prevented the other thing.

173

What?

MARION

The other thing. Eitel and me. I wanted Eitel. Then you came along. I wanted you. I wanted both of you.

ELENA

Were you insane?

MARION

Incest is always insane. But that's where the atomic power is buried, little boob. Incest, man, feedback, that's civilization. The mirror. Self-image, you ass, that's sanity, some image you can have of yourself. So bang me, mommy, dig.

(Stops. Considers. Stares at her.)

Besides, you bled the manhood from Eitel, you maggot.

ELENA

I didn't.

MARION

You bled my beloved Charley like a leech. Here . . . take the pills.

ELENA

How can you want this? I gave you more than I gave anyone.

MARION
(He says this angelically)
I know, sweetheart, but somehow I never did get to like your smell.

ELENA
(Swallows the pills)
There, it's done . . . I'm done.

MARION

You'll be asleep soon.

ELENA

You don't care.

174

MARION

I think you're great if you can hold out. I mean, like I
don't know if I can watch.

ELENA

You horror. You're not killer enough to kill the hate in
me.

MARION

Not killer enough. You squat. You eat the goodness from
your seed.

ELENA

For a moment I knew what it was. With Charley I knew.

MARION

And with me.

ELENA

And with you. I will go mad.

MARION

Die.

ELENA

The night I met Charley I was ready to cut my wrists.
Instead I went to bed with him. One last fling . . . I thought
a miracle had come. I wanted to live again.

MARION

Die. Drown in the Niagara of your sentimental shit.

ELENA

Charley and I had so far to go to meet each other, and
love is beautiful at the end of a long trip. Now I'll never
feel love anymore. Oh, Charley, forgive me, oh Charley,
forgive.

> (*Reaches for the phone, but the
> drug causes her difficulty in dialing.
> As she is about to dial the last num-
> ber, Marion takes the phone.*)

Maybe you are right to stop me. I have brought good to no
one.

175

(It is the only self-admission which could save her. The avenging angel within Marion delivers its verdict: the execution will not take place.)

MARION
(Voice filled with hatred of himself for capitulating)

It seems I have a drop of mercy after all.

(Dials the last number)

ELENA
(Into the phone in a listless voice)
Charley . . . I took some pills. . . . Please call the hospital. . . . Send an ambulance over here . . . to Marion's.

(Hangs up)

I'm sorry, Marion. I'm so sorry, but I don't want to stop.

(She begins to weep.

It is at this moment that the BOMB goes off a hundred miles away—far across the desert.

The light through the window is intense, a white shuddering light. Elena screams, and Marion does not move.)

CHANGE EIGHT

MARION
(Over the high piercing note of the bomb's explosion, high and piercing as the wail of a jet engine)

The bomb, my friends, yes, let it come. Let this explosion

come, and then another, and all the others. Let it come and clear the rot and the stench and the stink, let it come for all of everywhere, just so it comes and the world stands clear in the white dead dawn.

(Silence—the echo of the bomb is gone)

Dorothea, my mother, she took money from men when I was young. I was a bastard, a passing gift from a passing prince. Yes, I was her bastard. I grew up while she was writing her gossip column, the cruellest gossip columnist in the country, an assassin. She used to print the American flag next to her face, so I knew what it was all about, I mean I knew early. She wanted me to be a priest—I was to be her sacrifice.

. . . Do I have to spell it out? I have this idea so deep in my head—

(Striking his forehead)

that the center of Hell must be in here, yes, I have this idea that I am a saint, and I feel what God feels, and He is in a desperation beyond mine because there is an extraordinary destiny He has to achieve and He does not know whether He will succeed or not because He is a part of us. He is failing because we are failing, because we are too cowardly, because we want to move slowly, and hold to what we have, when the world, the tangible substance of God, is ready to be blown beyond existence in those radiations of hate which none of us can contain any longer. There is a torment coming when the being of all of us will depend on whether there is a man brave enough, bold enough, to go further in his mind than anyone has ever gone and yet communicate his vision. And I am not that man. I am too weak. I have failed God again.

(Light fades. In the darkness there is the wail of an ambulance coming closer and closer.)

177

CHANGE SEVEN

ELENA

Charley, you better go. I know how you hate hospitals.

EITEL

I'll stay. I don't like to think of you being alone here.

ELENA

Oh, Charley, marry me, please marry me.

(He does not answer)

You feel cold as stone, don't you?

EITEL

No. It's just that you made me cry. You're the only woman who's ever made me cry more than once. So, yes, let's get married. Your wounds soothe my wounds. I think that's better than to be alone.

ELENA

Oh, Charley, say something more than that.

EITEL

Not yet.

(Lights fade)

(Lights up. A spot on Sergius holding an empty bottle in his hand. He looks haggard and his manner is subdued.)

SERGIUS

The worst is over. We enter now on a plain of domesticity. In Hell, like Life, the years pass into the years, and we count our time in lonely private rhythms which have little to

178

do with number or judgment or the uncertain shifting memory of friends.

(A conjuror's gesture)

For instance, the ghosts of my beloved Lulu and Charles Francis Eitel . . .

CHANGE SIX

(Lights on Eitel's living room as Lulu runs in)

LULU

Charley, don't scold. I'm in a state.

EITEL

Lulu, child, we really don't have too much time. Elena could get here very soon.

LULU

Charley, would you mind if we let things go for tonight?

EITEL

Yes, I've spent too much of this week figuring out how to smuggle in a few hours with you.

LULU

Charley, there's a crisis on.

EITEL

A crisis?

LULU

Tony's in trouble. He beat up a waitress in a restaurant in Cleveland.

EITEL

That is a mess.

LULU

It's terrible. . . . Why does the studio send him out on personal appearances? They ought to keep him in a cage. My press agent is in a panic. He says if I make the wrong move, this could finish my career.

EITEL

More probably, it'll finish Tony.

LULU

Tony's the hottest property in town. The studio has to save him. Don't you see they're going to spread the story that I drove Tony to it because I'm a bad wife.

EITEL

Supreme can't afford to sacrifice you.

LULU

The hell they can't. Tony is bigger than me.

EITEL

Don't scream, Lulu.

LULU

I'm sorry.

EITEL

Doesn't your press agent have any ideas?

LULU

Oh, Monroney is useless. He thinks I should make a statement that Tony's brutal, and I know exactly what the waitress went through, and so forth and so forth.

EITEL

People won't like it.

LULU

Of course they won't. But Monroney says that's the best I can do. His theory is: I have to attack before Supreme attacks me. I can't think straight. I'm so wound up, Charley. Please help me.

EITEL

It's a mistake to fight Supreme's publicity. They're too

180

strong for you.

> LULU
> *(With exasperation)*

I know they are.

> EITEL

But they don't want to lose you unless they have to. If you make it possible, Supreme will be happy to save Tony and you.

> LULU

Charley, be specific.

> EITEL

I can work it out right now. . . . Call the airport and make a reservation to Cleveland.

> *(He gestures toward the bedroom. She dashes toward it, stops, turns.)*

> LULU

Ohio?

> *(Eitel waves her on. While Lulu is offstage, Eitel opens his typewriter case and begins to type. Mumbling to himself, he tries out the sound, reading some of the words aloud. As he finishes, Lulu, done with her call, comes back, and reads over his shoulder. They finish together.)*

> EITEL

Miss Meyers said today, "It's all my fault. Tony must not be blamed. I feel terrible about that poor wretch . . . poor waitress . . . emotional and psychological difficulties . . . even more than me."

> LULU
> *(Hugs him)*

Charley, you're a great man. When I'm in Cleveland, can I phone you here if I need advice?

EITEL

I guess so. I'll find some explanation for Elena.

LULU

She's jealous, isn't she?

EITEL

Sometimes.

LULU

Charles, are you happy with Elena?

EITEL

I'm not unhappy. Victor sometimes gives me great pleasure.

LULU

I never could have thought of you as a father.

EITEL

Neither could I. But I love that baby.

LULU

How do you know you love him?

EITEL

Because I want him to be better than me.

LULU

Oh, Charley, I love you an awful lot. Do you know you have real dignity now?

EITEL

It's nice of you to say that, Lulu. . . . You know, I wouldn't want this to get around, and I don't suppose I've told it to anyone in years, but my mother was a French maid before she married my father. Of course, she worked only in the best homes.

LULU

Oh, Charley, Charley, why didn't you ever know . . . that you were my big love? Come on, let's go over to my place before I take the plane. You look good enough to eat. Ugh, Cleveland!

(Blackout)

182

CHANGE FIVE

(In the dark we hear the voice of a television announcer)

ANNOUNCER

Reached at Los Angeles International Airport, Miss Lulu Meyers in an exclusive and confidential interview said today . . .

(Sound of flashbulbs, paparazzi, tumult. Spot on Lulu. She is wearing a white fur stole)

LULU

It's all my fault. Tony must not be blamed. I feel terrible about that poor waitress and I know Tony feels even worse. But the emotional and psychological difficulties that led Tony to commit such an act are all of my making. Down deep, Tony has a wonderful character, but I've failed to give him the love and unselfishness he needs, although in my own cockeyed childish way, I love him very much. Perhaps, out of this trouble, which is my responsibility more than Tony's, I will achieve the maturity and humility I've been looking for so long. I'm flying to Cleveland right away to be with Tony, and I hope that out of all this something good may come for Tony even more than me.

CHANGE FOUR

(Lights on Eitel's Desert D'Or patio. Elena paces, waiting. Eitel enters and she runs to him.)

ELENA

Where have you been?

183

EITEL

I got tired of waiting for you, and I went out to have a drink.

ELENA

You mean you've been with a girl.

EITEL

Elena, let's not get into that again. It was your idea to come out here, and I went through a good bit of trouble to get exactly our old love-nest reserved.

ELENA

It doesn't mean a thing to you.

EITEL

Baby, this is a vacation. Let's not fight on our first evening. I had to be up at six this morning. I was at the studio at eight. I was obliged to work with my cutter on that last miserable clinker I turned out. Let's start this evening over again. Imagine I just came through the door. And I say to you—how did you spend the morning?

ELENA

I played bridge with Lottie Munshin.

EITEL

Fine.

ELENA

I hate bridge.

EITEL

What's really the matter, Elena?

ELENA

I saw my analyst this morning.

EITEL

Well, now I understand.

ELENA

Yes, I know, it's very funny. But I had a fight with my analyst.

EITEL

Well, it's probably worth fifty dollars an hour to fight with somebody besides me.

ELENA

My analyst told me I was regressing, being childish, paranoid attitude toward you, sign of a weak ego. . . . I don't know what happened, Charley, but I started screaming at him, and I told him that nobody was asking him to take my money and . . . finally I told him he was not attractive enough to understand me.

EITEL

Well, if you said that, he'll be a patient himself soon.

ELENA

I don't want the kind of life he thinks I should have.

EITEL

What do you mean?

ELENA

Charley, we have the baby, and we'll probably have another baby, and I have good relations with the servants, and I do love the dancing classes, and I love you, I really think I still love you, but, Charley, is that enough? Is Vickie enough? I mean did we go through . . . what we went through . . . just so I could rise from being a poor wop to being a nice rich neurotic housewife?

EITEL

Sweetheart . . . you've grown more than anybody in the time I've known you.

ELENA

I can't talk to you unless you'll understand. When I was younger . . . I used to think . . . there was something beautiful in me. I can't say how. I used to feel such lovely things. In secrecy I used to think that if I could find my man, he would lift me out of ignorance and dirt, and I would travel anywhere with him, with any man who was brave enough to keep my love alive, brave enough to live

185

with my cruel and greedy blood. But it hasn't been that
way. Everyone I know is getting dead and dull.

> *(Eitel, the husband, fills the pause*
> *in his wife's statement)*

EITEL

I'm not the only one who killed the sex in you. There was
another. You never stopped thinking of him.

ELENA

I haven't thought of him in years. We avoid the subject, my
analyst and me. But this I haven't told you, I got a telegram
from Marion this morning. He's coming out of prison
and he thinks he will be by to see me. Do you know.
Charley, that I felt a lift of hope for the first moment in
I don't know how many months.

EITEL

The devil is the most beautiful creature God ever made.

ELENA

Didn't you hear? I hope that Marion comes to see me.

EITEL

Yes, I hear you. You tell me that Marion traveled into
a part of you I have never known.

ELENA

It was the marijuana, my analyst said.

EITEL

Who cares what it was? I'm tired to the bone and my
heart beats bad.

ELENA

Will you be silent about exhaustions you bring to me from
other women?

EITEL

I am weary unto death—I confess it.

ELENA

You are boring.

EITEL

You are murderous in your stupidity. Oh, baby, once and again, whenever it happens, I still love to give it to you, that's the simple truth. It wasn't all wasted, Elena. I never knew what it was all about, until I learned from you.

ELENA

But I didn't learn from you.

EITEL
(Pause)

Yes, you are cruel.

ELENA

Your coldness is now in me. I think my breasts are losing their shape.

EITEL

It is because you were too selfish to feed the baby for more than a month.

ELENA

Good night, Charley. Hope you had a good screw this afternoon.

EITEL

I've had worse.

ELENA

Drop dead!

(She starts to walk off stage, then her fury brings her back)

Die!

(Eitel is left alone)

187

CHANGE THREE

(The lights alter and go down until there is only a modest illumination on Eitel. A suggestion of music springs up from somewhere but it is vague, like a wisp of fog, now a wisp and all too soon a vapor. "Sergius?" Eitel calls.)

EITEL

Sergius, what does one ever do with one's life? Are you one of those who know? For I do not. It is the mark of my life that the forgotten memory of your face is all that is left, a casual friend I hardly knew, and yet I like you. Yes, now I see your face.

(Eitel's hand comes to his breast as if he suffers a sudden unmistakable pain)

Aiiiiihhhh, the clot of unborn rage at all I have not done and all that I will never do . . . it tears now at my heart, and I am going to die . . . but where I go, ah, there's the fright—I do not know—it may be for worse.

(Slowly Eitel slips to the floor, the light disappears on him and as it does, Elena finds him in the darkness, gives a wail, cries out)

CHANGE TWO

ELENA

What have I done? He meant it when he said he was weary. May God have mercy on me.

188

(Then she kneels over his body; the sound of her sobbing)

SERGIUS

And she was left alone to live with this, for her man was gone, the poor man went of that disease which goes by so many names, that law of life so cruel and so just that we must grow or else pay more for remaining the same. And, as he died, his spirit passed on to me, for to pass on one's spirit is the one small gift we are allowed in Hell, and if there are enough to care for us, we can enter your world again—which is why perhaps we have spent this most curious evening watching the damned chase after love.

CHANGE ONE

ELENA

(Elena looks up. Her hands are still on Eitel's body.)

His coldness is now in me, but my death ended him. What fear I know of Hell for the other voice says I shall be stronger now.

(Marion appears. He is older—a measure of the time he has spent in prison is on his face.)

MARION

Nobility and vice—they're the same thing—When you come to the end of one, you are ready to discover the other.

(He walks past Elena, and touches her enigmatically on the forehead. As he exits, she follows him. Perhaps his touch is not altogether enigmatic, perhaps it speaks of that monologue when he had struck his own forehead and declared that "the center of Hell must be in here.")

SERGIUS

Now, armed with the gift of my old friend's bequest, there are hours when in this loneliness I would have the anger to call upon the Lord Himself, and I would ask, "Would You agree that Sex is where the vision begins?" But I think that God would answer only, "Rather think of Sex as Time and Time the connection of new circuits." "Connection of new . . . circuits . . . ?" I say, and must add, "Sir, isn't Time rather the capture of conception?" "Connection of new circuits is good enough for an American with a mechanical head like yours," the Lord roars back in my ear. Then for a moment in that cold Irish soul of mine a glimmer of the joy of the flesh comes back to me, rare as the eye of the rarest tear of compassion, and we laugh together after all, for to hear that Sex is Time and Time the connection of new circuits is a part of the poor odd dialogues which give hope to us noble humans for more than one night.

The prologue is over, the body is

190

done, the epilogue has begun.

(A wink)

Stop necking in the rear.

(A pleasant grin, a hint that the next hour will be more merry than the last)

Good night.

(The lights go down)

NORMAN MAILER'S

The Deer Park

was produced in New York by Supreme Pix, Inc.
(Garen-Mailer-Walsh)
and had its premiere performance, Tuesday, January 31, 1967
at the Theatre De Lys, New York City

THE ORIGINAL CAST
(in order of appearance)

SERGIUS O'SHAUGNESSY—*An Air Force Flyer*   Gene Lindsey

MARION FAYE—*A Pimp*   Rip Torn

BOBBY—*A Call Girl*   Marsha Mason

LULU MEYERS—*A Movie Star*   Beverly Bentley

CHARLES FRANCIS EITEL—*A Movie Director*   Hugh Marlowe

CARLYLE MUNSHIN—*A Movie Producer*   Mickey Knox

TEPPIS—*Head of Supreme Pix*   Will Lee

ELENA ESPOSITO—*A Dancer*   Rosemary Tory

TEDDY POPE—*A Movie Star*   Joe McWherter

TONY TUNNER—*An Actor*   Gary Campbell

DOROTHEA O'FAYE—*A Gossip Columnist*   Margaret Fairchild

DON BEDA—*A Millionaire*   Bernard Farbar

ZENLIA—*Model, Mistress of Kings*   Mara Lynn

DIRECTED BY *Leo Garen*

PRODUCED BY *James Walsh*

SETTING AND LIGHTING BY	COSTUMES BY	MUSIC SUPERVISED BY
Will Steven Armstrong	*Ann Roth*	*Charles Gross*

PRODUCTION STAGE MANAGER, *Paul John Austin*

Presented by Special Arrangement with
LUCILLE LORTEL PRODUCTIONS, INC.